I0555246

The Day Walker: Balancing Light and Shadow on the Path to Awakening

BY

MIZDEN MARTINEZ

Copyright © 2025 by Mizden Martinez

All rights reserved. No part of this publication may be reproduced, stored or transmitted in any form or by any means, electronic, mechanical, photocopying, recording, scanning, or otherwise without written permission from the publisher. It is illegal to copy this book, post it to a website, or distribute it by any other means without permission.

Preface

For years, I walked a path that felt like both a mystery and a calling. As a lightworker, grid worker, blueprint holder, shaman, and starseed, my life has been an intricate dance between worlds—the seen and unseen, the light and the shadow. Each role brought with it lessons, challenges, and profound spiritual growth, allowing me to transcend. Altough this has been my life's journey, it wasn't until recently, during a trance with my shaman drum, that a term emerged to encapsulate my journey: Day Walker.

A Day Walker isn't just a name or an idea; it's a way of being. It is the bridge between realms, a role that harmonizes the human experience with divine purpose. It's about bringing the wisdom of the spiritual into the physical world, illuminating spaces where darkness once thrived, and inspiring transformation. This revelation felt like a missing piece of my identity, a word that finally gave shape to the life I have always lived.

I am writing this book because I believe that the Day Walker path holds the transformative power to make a significant difference in the world. This path is not merely a journey; it is a profound spiritual calling that resonates deep within our souls, offering the potential to awaken hidden abilities in others and inspire them to embark on their own unique journeys. Each of us carries a light within that, when nurtured, can illuminate the way for those around us. By sharing my story, I hope to ignite a spark in those who resonate with these truths—whether you are a starseed seeking to understand your cosmic origins, a healer dedicated to facilitating growth and transformation, a seeker on a quest for deeper knowledge, or simply someone yearning to connect with something greater than yourself. Together, we can cultivate a community of like-minded souls, each embracing their individuality while contributing to the collective consciousness. My hope is that through this exploration of the Day Walker path, you will find inspiration and encouragement to honor your own journey and the unique gifts you bring to the world.

This book is not just about me. It's about the collective shift in consciousness that occurs when we embrace our higher purpose. It's about the energy grids we align, the light we hold, and the healing we inspire when we choose to walk in balance between worlds. My hope is that as you turn these pages, you will feel a ripple of inspiration, a call to your own awakening, and a reminder that your light contributes to something far beyond yourself.

The Day Walker path is about integration: the shadow and the light, the mundane and the divine, the self and the collective. It's about bringing the extraordinary into the everyday. This book is my offering to those who feel called to walk a similar path—a guide, a companion, and a testament to the power of embracing who you truly are.

Let this journey be an invitation to grow, transform, and shine as brightly as the world needs you to. The Day Walker exists to make a difference. Together, we can create a wave of change, one soul at a time.

With love and light,

Mizden

Acknowledgement

To my children, for their patience and love as I poured my heart into these pages. Thank you for holding space for me.

To the friends who may not even realize the impact they've had-Marissa Miller, Derek Badonie, Ryan McLean, and some guy. You each, in your own way, reminded me I wasn't alone-through laughter, silence, or simply existing nearby when I needed it most. Your presence helped me breathe easier and find the courage to keep going.

To Shaun White, my guiding light and dearest friend. Shai, who walked alongside me on this journey with unwavering support and profound wisdom. Your role as my shaman, Shaman Om, transcended the ordinary, you helped me navigate the depths of my soul, illuminating paths I never knew existed. Thank you for your steadfast belief in me and for teaching me the power of love and healing. Your presence in my life has been a gift that will forever resonate in my heart.

And lastly, to the Universe, for aligning every moment, lesson, and challenge to bring me here.

With deep gratitude,

Mizden Martinez

THE DAY WALKER: BALANCING LIGHT AND SHADOW ON THE PATH TO AWAKENING

For the Seeker-

The one who dares to look within, who walks through darkness in search of light, who falls, questions, unravels, and still chooses to rise.

This is for you.

May these words remind you that you are never alone.

Table of Contents

Introduction

The Path of a Day Walker

I am a Day Walker, a soul who moves gently between light and shadow. I seek not to conquer one, or escape the other, but to find harmony in their eternal dance, a cosmic dance. I do not see duality as a conflict to resolve, but as a truth to honor—two forces shaping the world and my own journey. Light does not exist without shadow, and shadow does not exist without light. I walk between them, embracing both; they are one.

Yet, to be a Day Walker is to be neither wholly of the sun nor fully of the night. I exist in the in-between, a liminal current where time bends and veils thin. My spirit is stretched across realms, drawn by whispers of ancient knowledge, by symbols left behind in forgotten tongues. I close my eyes, and I see the golden pulse of energy between all things, the shifting tide of fate, the echoes of souls who have long since left this world—a delicate symphony. I do not merely live in the present; I live in what was, what is, and what could be, all woven together like threads of an unseen tapestry, a timeless place not bound to its very own existence.

I am called, time and again, into visions—some familiar,

some foreign. They flicker like candlelight in the corridors of my mind, pulling me into depths that others fear to tread. The winds speak to me in languages that were never taught but are always known. The earth hums with wisdom, waiting for those who can hear. I have walked through dreams that feel more real than waking life, touched truths too vast to name, and stood at the edge of mysteries that no human tongue could ever fully shape.

Hour by hour, I work to maintain this balance, knowing that harmony is not a prize to be won but a rhythm to be felt. It is a process—fluid, ever changing, requiring strength, discipline, and surrender. Some days, I find myself basking in the warmth of clarity, feeling aligned with purpose and certainty. Other days, I am swallowed by uncertainty, lost in the fog of doubt. When anger rises, I do not silence it; I sit with it, listening to what it reveals about my boundaries. When grief weighs heavy, I do not push it away; I let it carve space for deeper love. When fear whispers of failure, I do not run; I face it and learn its name.

I do not fear the darkness when it arrives. Instead, I stand firm and observe. Like a mirror, it reflects truths I might otherwise ignore. I embrace it; in return, it does not threaten me—it teaches me. I have learned that challenges are not meant to break us, but to shape us. Each trial is an invitation to grow, to deepen, to understand. I do not resist these lessons, nor do I pretend that pain does not exist. I embrace it, not as suffering, but as alchemy the transformation of the soul is no different from the transmutation of lead to gold. It requires pressure, heat, and time. And through that process, I illuminate my own path and inspire others to do the same.

But I do not walk this path for myself alone. I am a bridge between extremes, a guide for those still trapped in the illusions of division. I help others break free from the weight of limiting beliefs—the ones they inherited, the ones they built for themselves, the ones that keep them from seeing that they are more than their fears. I remind them that life's burdens are not punishments but invitations—doorways to something greater.

Yet, this is not the only thing that sets me apart. I am not bound by one path, nor confined to a single role. I am a seeker, a healer, a storyteller, a guardian of forgotten wisdom. I have walked roads unknown, carrying truths that cannot be shared, and words that cannot be spoken—only felt. I have stood in the stillness of ancient echoes, where time folds in on itself, where the past and future whisper secrets to those willing to listen. My existence is not defined solely by my ability to walk between light and shadow, but by my capacity to adapt, to transform, to become whatever the moment demands.

I am not just a Day Walker. I am a force of change, a keeper of lost knowledge, a traveler between what is seen and what is felt. I am shaped by experience, by the weight of my choices, by the silent forces that move through me. And even as I embrace this path, I know there is always more to discover, more to learn, more to become.

I do not exist to fit within boundaries—I exist to transcend them. As a Day Walker, I am a spiritually empowered being who embraces the totality of existence, gently navigating the delicate dance of life's polarities, much like the harmonious interplay of yin and yang. I strive to be a compassionate beacon of balance, illuminating the path for others to accept and love every facet of themselves—both the light and the shadow. For instance, when I encounter someone struggling with self-doubt, I share my own moments of uncertainty, reminding them that even the brightest lights cast shadows.

Through the transformative practice of shadow work, I invite others to embark on their journeys of self-discovery and healing, encouraging them to confront their hidden aspects with kindness and understanding. I've witnessed the profound shifts that occur when individuals embrace their fears and insecurities. In one instance, a friend faced her fear of rejection by expressing her true feelings to someone she cared about; that courageous step not only strengthened her spirit but also opened up a dialogue of vulnerability that deepened our connection.

This process becomes a powerful catalyst for spiritual growth, allowing individuals to transcend their limitations and connect more deeply with their true selves. I deeply recognize that true enlightenment does not come from rejecting any part of ourselves; instead, it emerges from weaving together all of our experiences and emotions into a beautiful tapestry of wholeness. I recall a time when I reflected on my own past mistakes and, instead of feeling shame, I embraced them as essential chapters in my story. By accepting those parts of myself, I found a newfound strength that propelled me forward.

By walking in truth and authenticity, I empower those around me to acknowledge their inherent worth, fostering a nurturing community where we can all grow and thrive. When I share my story of transformation, I see others light up with the realization that they, too, can embrace their unique journeys. In this sacred space, we inspire one another to nurture connections rooted in empathy and understanding. Together, we contribute to the collective evolution of consciousness, creating a ripple effect of love, healing, and transformation that transcends individual boundaries and uplifts our entire community.

For example, when I facilitate group discussions on personal growth, I encourage participants to share their stories. The room fills with the energy of shared experiences, where one person's vulnerability inspires another to open up, leading to collective healing. Each story becomes a thread in our communal tapestry, reminding us that we are never alone on this path.

Psychological Aspect of the Day Walker; Walking between the realms of light and shadow requires a mind shaped by resilience, deep self-awareness, and an openness to the complexities of existence. As a Day Walker, I embody the duality of life, acting as a bridge between illumination and obscurity. This role is more than just a title; it's an intricate psychological journey, a constant dialogue between opposites that challenges me to navigate the nuances of my existence. I confront not only the external shadows of humanity but also the deeply personal ones that linger within me, often surfacing in the quiet moments of introspection. This process takes immense courage, as I face my fears, doubts, and the parts of myself I've tried to suppress over time.

The journey isn't linear or tidy; it often feels like madness, an immersion into chaos that unravels everything familiar and predictable in my life. At times, it can feel disorienting, almost like psychosis, derealization, or depersonalization, where the lines between my inner and outer worlds blur and fracture. In those moments, I find myself questioning the very fabric of reality, grappling with the unsettling sensations that arise. Yet, amid this turmoil, I have to find my anchor—a calm within the storm—and discover a strange beauty in the chaos itself. It's through embracing this wild, unpredictable path that I find not just survival but also the profound power of transformation, where each moment of chaos becomes an opportunity for growth.

The psychological demands of being a Day Walker extend beyond mere resilience into the realms of emotional intelligence, surrender, and radical acceptance of chaos. I don't view darkness—grief, anger, confusion, and loss—as an enemy to be vanquished but rather as a teacher and guide. These emotions hold valuable lessons, urging me to befriend them, understand them, and accept them without judgment. This perspective allows me to sit with my pain, not as something to fix or eliminate but as a state to comprehend and even embrace. It requires a delicate balance; darkness has a way of distorting reality, pulling me into states where the familiar feels strange and where my sense of self may become fragmented, leaving me feeling unmoored, lacking contact with reality.

In those moments of fragmentation, I consciously resist the urge to retreat or numb myself. Instead, I breathe through the disorientation, allowing it to reshape me rather than tear me apart, becoming friends with dissociative moments while I embrace the "in-between." Each storm I weather teaches me to find calm in the eye of the storm, to appreciate beauty not in perfection but in the raw, untamed chaos of existence. Through this alchemical process, I come to realize that what feels like madness is often the doorway to a deeper understanding of myself and the world, revealing the unknown and the hidden aspects of my being that yearn for acknowledgment.

Embracing this madness without losing myself takes immense strength and discipline. I learn to dance in the void, finding harmony in the tension between creation and destruction, finding beauty in chaos. I discover the potential for rebirth within moments of disarray, trusting that even in my darkest moments, there is purpose and meaning waiting to be unveiled. By moving through these states of seeming disorder and disconnection, I reclaim a sense of unity and wholeness, integrating the lessons learned from both light and shadow into my being.

In this journey, I recognize that I am not a savior but a guide, embodying the paradox of calm within chaos. My existence serves as a living testament that transformation isn't about avoiding darkness but mastering it. Through my experiences, I hope to inspire others to embrace their own journeys, understanding that the path of the Day Walker is not just about traversing the realms of light and shadow but about embracing the richness of life in all its complexities.

Chapter 1 Embracing the Shadow

Understanding my Shadow Self; For a long time, I believed the parts of me that I tried to hide were flaws. I believed they were things I needed to bury deep to fit into the world around me. These parts felt like shadows, lurking quietly in the corners of my mind, unacknowledged but never truly absent. Over time, I began working on myself, driven by a need to understand the emotions and patterns that seemed to hold me back. I didn't have a name for what I was doing, but the process felt deeply transformative, like I was peeling back layers of myself I had forgotten existed and gaining the opportunity to become more.

Then, one day, Shaman Om asked me if I had done shadow work. Being unfamiliar with the term "shadow work," I asked what it entailed. He simply responded, "Look into it, so you can find your way. It's not something I can teach you, it's something you must learn on your own terms in order for it to guide you and actually work." Intrigued, I did a quick search and discovered that shadow work was not only a real concept but a practice that resonated with everything I had already been doing. It was like finding the missing puzzle piece that tied my efforts together. I had the action, not the words. Seeing that this process had been explored and practiced by others strengthened my views and motivated me to dive even deeper. I realized I had been scratching the surface, but now I was ready to get to the root of everything with a level of depth I hadn't reached before.

Spiritually, the shadow represents the unconscious side of us, the parts we suppress because they don't align with the image we present to the world—like taboos. But this darkness isn't something to fear. In many traditions, it's seen as a necessary counterpart to the light. Taoism, for example, teaches that yin and yang—the dark and the light—exist in harmony, each essential to the other. Even alchemy, with its ancient symbols and mystical processes, reflects this idea. Transforming base metals into gold mirrors the journey of turning our hidden, unresolved self into something profound and whole.

Psychologically, I learned about the shadow through the work of Carl Jung. He described it as the unconscious mind's hidden aspects, shaped by the experiences and societal expectations that teach us what is "acceptable." As children, we may hear, "Don't be so angry," or, "Stop being so sensitive," and those parts of us get tucked away, labeled as "wrong." And so, we begin to suppress parts of our identity. But the shadow doesn't disappear just because we've ignored it. Instead, it shows up in subtle ways, perhaps in the traits we dislike in others or the emotional barriers we can't seem to overcome.

For me, shadow work has been about asking myself hard questions: Why do certain people trigger me? Why do I feel uncomfortable with certain emotions? Why do I imagine events that aren't happening? Each answer has pointed me back to a piece of myself I tried to disown, **to** reject. It's not easy work.

Confronting the shadow is like holding up a mirror and seeing not just the person I want to be but also the person I've hidden away.

As I explored this further, I discovered that the concept of the shadow isn't new. It's woven into the spiritual and philosophical teachings of countless traditions. In Hinduism and Buddhism, there's an emphasis on transcending attachments and desires—things that obscure the true self. Shamanic practices involve confronting fears and healing fragmented parts of the soul, which sounds a lot like shadow work to me. Even in Western philosophy, Plato's allegory of the cave hints at this idea of hidden truths waiting to be uncovered.

Jung's perspective, though, resonates deeply with me. He didn't see the shadow as something to fight against but as a guide—a bridge to our true self. The more I've embraced this, the more I've realized that the shadow holds not only my fears but also my untapped potential. It's where my creativity lives, where my authenticity waits to shine through.

Shadow work has become a journey of self-compassion. It's about learning to sit with myself, even when I'm uncomfortable, and saying, "You're still worthy." It's not about fixing or changing these parts of me, it's about accepting them and recognizing the balance they bring to my life. The shadow is as much a part of me as the light, and together, they make me whole.

The more I explored my shadow self, the more I realized that the darkness wasn't inherently evil, but it was still terrifying. It was hard to look into the mirror it held, to see the parts of me I didn't want to face. Darkness isn't where I found comfort or clarity, it's where I found resistance, fear, and truth all tangled together. But I chose to remain neutral, steadying myself to face it for what it was, rather than what I feared it might be.

I learned to accept the shadow because I realized the light cannot exist without the dark. As Martin Luther King Jr. said, "Only in the darkness can you see the stars." Those words helped me find meaning in my struggle. The stars—

the truths about myself, my potential, and my wholeness—couldn't shine in the glare of avoidance or denial. It was only by stepping into the shadows, holding my own hand, that I could begin to truly see.

The shadow is as much a part of me as the light, and together, they make me whole. But understanding this wasn't easy. I had to look deeper, not just at myself but at how the world around me shaped the darkness I carried. After all, societal conditioning and trauma contribute to shadow creation.

So much of my shadow was born from the expectations and judgments placed on me by society. From a young age, I learned what was "acceptable" and what wasn't. Society has a way of teaching us to hide parts of ourselves, to be strong, quiet, agreeable, or whatever else fits its idea of "normal." Vulnerability was seen as weakness. Anger was labeled as destructive. Even ambition could be "too much." I didn't question it then. I just buried those parts of me, hoping it would make me more acceptable, more lovable. But those parts never went away—they just hid in the shadows, waiting for me to face them.

Trauma only made the shadow grow. When I experienced rejection, pain, or shame, my instinct was to protect myself by hiding even more. I shoved away my vulnerability, joy, and even my need for connection because they felt too risky to show. Trauma taught me to compartmentalize, to lock away the parts of myself that hurt or felt unsafe. But those emotions—anger, fear, shame—didn't disappear.

They just lingered in the dark, waiting for the day I could finally acknowledge them. It wasn't until I started shadow work that I realized how much of my darkness wasn't truly mine. It was shaped by what I was taught to suppress and the pain I'd been too afraid to face. Darkness wasn't my enemy; it was the contrast that gave the light its meaning. In those moments of quiet acceptance, not fighting or running, I began to see the balance. The shadow is as much a part of me as the light, and together, they make me whole.

The more I've leaned into this process, the more I've felt a profound sense of freedom. The shadow isn't my enemy, it's my teacher, showing me the way to the parts of myself I've been too afraid to face. By embracing it, I'm learning to step into the fullness of who I am, finding harmony between the seen and unseen, the light and the dark.

How Society and Trauma shaped My Shadow? I used to think my shadow was just my own, a personal vault of hidden fears, suppressed desires, and unspoken pain. I believed it was the result of my own mistakes, a byproduct of experiences I didn't fully process. But the more I worked through it, the more I realized that my shadow wasn't just mine. It was shaped by the world around me, by unseen forces stretching far beyond my own life. The way I viewed myself, the things I suppressed, and the emotions I buried weren't entirely personal, they were echoes of the expectations, rules, and wounds imposed on me. I inherited my shadow as much as I created it, and in many ways, I had been carrying pieces of pain that were never truly mine to begin with.

From the moment we enter the world, we begin learning the unspoken rules of what is acceptable and what is not. These rules aren't written down, but they are enforced in glances, in silences, in the way love is given and withheld. I learned quickly that some emotions were welcome, while others were met with discomfort. If I expressed sadness too openly, I was seen as weak. If I questioned authority, I was labeled difficult. If I showed too much ambition, I was met with warnings about humility. And so, without ever consciously deciding to, I began trimming parts of myself away, shrinking who I was.

Maybe you've done the same. Maybe you've felt the quiet sting of rejection when you expressed yourself too freely. Maybe you've learned to shrink in certain spaces, to swallow your words, to apologize for taking up too much room, feeling like you're "too much." The world conditions us to be palatable, easy to swallow, to fit within an acceptable range of expression. Anything outside that range—anything too wild, too intense, too unpredictable— gets pushed into the shadows. Not because it's wrong, but because it makes others uncomfortable. And so, we exile parts of ourselves, believing that doing so will make us safer, more loved, and ultimately, accepted.

But not all of our shadows are formed in our lifetime. Some of them are passed down. Generational trauma is more than just a phrase—it's a lived experience that we carry in our bodies, in our beliefs, in the way we navigate the world. I used to think I was just naturally anxious, that my fear of scarcity or my hyper-vigilance was just a personal trait. But then I looked deeper. I saw how my ancestors survived war, displacement, oppression, how their fear of losing everything wasn't paranoia but a reality they lived through. That fear didn't die with them; it lived on in the way my family viewed the world, in the lessons they taught me without even realizing it.

Maybe your family passed down resilience, or maybe they passed down silence. Maybe they handed you strength, or maybe they unknowingly gave you fear. We inherit more than just genetics. We inherit pain, survival mechanisms, and coping strategies that may no longer serve us. The weight of unprocessed trauma doesn't just fade; it lingers in the way we carry ourselves, in the patterns we repeat without knowing why. And unless we stop to examine it, we live our lives burdened by ghosts of wounds that were never ours to bear.

The earliest architects of our shadow are often the people closest to us—our families. The messages we receive in childhood become the foundation of how we see ourselves, and for many of us, that foundation is built on unspoken expectations, on conditional love, on the quiet yet powerful pressure to be a certain way. It becomes our environment.

Maybe you were raised in a home where perfection was the standard, where mistakes weren't just mistakes but failures. Maybe love felt earned rather than given freely, so you learned to over-perform, to achieve, to prove yourself worthy. Or maybe emotions weren't welcomed at all, maybe anger was met with punishment, sadness with dismissal. And so, you learned to bury those feelings, to present only the parts of yourself that were deemed acceptable. Just because something is buried doesn't mean it disappears. Those suppressed emotions linger in the body, resurfacing in unexpected ways: anxiety, self-doubt, patterns of self-sabotage. The shadow never stays hidden forever.

It's not just our families, it's the systems we grow up in. Schools teach conformity, rewarding obedience over curiosity. They encourage memorization over independent thought, shaping us to follow the structure rather than question it. The education system, in many ways, molds us into digestible versions of ourselves, teaching us that fitting in is more important than standing out.

Religion, too, plays a role in shaping our shadows. Many of us were raised with rigid ideas of good and evil, right and wrong. We were told that certain desires were sinful, that questioning too much was dangerous, that suffering was noble. And so, we internalized shame, believing that normal human emotions—desire, anger, ambition—were things to be repressed rather than understood. This suppression doesn't erase those emotions; it forces them into the shadows, where they fester, waiting for the moment they'll break through in ways we can't control.

Even now, in a world that claims to celebrate authenticity, we are still conditioned to curate ourselves. Social media tells us who to be, what is likable, what is worthy of attention, what will be accepted, and sadly, a great deal of people follow without question. We present polished versions of ourselves, carefully constructed to avoid judgment. But behind the perfect posts and filtered images, the shadow grows.

We see it in the rise of anxiety, in the collective burnout, in the unspoken loneliness that lingers despite being more connected than ever. We are constantly performing, constantly editing ourselves to fit the expectations of others. But the more we suppress, the more we fracture. The shadow doesn't disappear; it waits. When it finally emerges, it often does so in ways that surprise even us: impulsive decisions, sudden anger, deep sadness that we can't quite explain.

Then there's trauma—the thing that doesn't just shape the shadow but sometimes fractures us entirely. When we go through something too painful to process, our minds do what they must to survive. We compartmentalize, we dissociate, we create versions of ourselves that can handle the pain while the rest of us goes into hiding. Some of us become perfectionists, believing that if we do everything right, we can avoid pain. Others become avoidant, detaching from emotions entirely. Some turn to control, others to self-destruction. But at the core of it all, trauma forces us to abandon parts of ourselves in order to cope.

And healing? Healing is the process of going back to

retrieve what was lost. So what now? If the shadow is built by society, by trauma, by generations of conditioning, how do we begin to reclaim ourselves? It starts with awareness—with asking hard questions about why we think, feel, and react the way we do. It means looking at our fears, our coping mechanisms, our deepest wounds, and asking: Is this truly mine? Or was this given to me? Introspection. The shadow isn't something to fear, it's something to understand. It's a map to the parts of ourselves that have been hidden for too long. When we bring it into the light, we don't just heal ourselves; we break cycles, we rewrite narratives, we make room for a version of ourselves that is whole, unfiltered, and free. And isn't that what we've been searching for all along?

Chapter 2 Walking through Darkness

Fear and struggle are universal experiences. They touch every part of our lives, often in ways we don't fully understand. From a spiritual perspective, these challenges aren't just obstacles to overcome, they're mirrors, reflecting the parts of ourselves we'd rather avoid. They stem from our shadow self, the hidden side of our psyche where suppressed fears, doubts, and pain reside. While the shadow often feels like an adversary, I've come to see it as a teacher, shaping me through every fear I face and every struggle I endure. The lessons aren't always easy to accept, but they're profound, transforming me into someone more resilient, self-aware, and whole. Each fear and struggle, though painful, has a purpose: to guide me closer to the truth of who I am.

One of the most profound fears I've faced is the fear of the unknown. There's something paralyzing about stepping into uncharted territory, whether it's starting a new chapter in life, entering a relationship, or diving deeper into my spiritual path. My shadow thrives in this space, whispering worst-case scenarios and pulling me back into the comfort of what I know. But as terrifying as it feels, I've come to realize that this fear shapes me. It forces me to let go of control and trust that clarity will eventually emerge from the chaos. The unknown is where growth happens, even if the shadow fights to keep me in the dark.

Rejection is another fear that has shaped me deeply. The pain of not being accepted or feeling unworthy used to consume me. It's as if my shadow constantly sought proof that I didn't belong or wasn't enough. Over time, I've come to see how much of my self-worth was tied to external validation. This fear taught me a profound lesson: I needed to turn inward and cultivate self-love. Rejection, I've learned, isn't always a sign of my inadequacy, but often a mirror showing me parts of myself that still need healing.

Self-doubt has been a constant struggle in my life. My inner critic is loud, questioning every step I take and every decision I make. My shadow thrives here, trying to convince me that I'm not capable or worthy of success. At first, I believed it, but eventually, I started to see how this struggle was shaping me. It was teaching me to pause and reflect, to question whether the voice of doubt was mine or something I'd absorbed from the world around me, from the environment. When I confront this doubt, I find inner strength and a quiet confidence that grows with each small victory.

The fear of failure is another shadow that has haunted me often. I've avoided risks, not because I didn't want success, but because I was terrified of falling short. For so long, failure felt like proof that I wasn't good enough. But the more I confronted this fear, the more I realized its power to shape me. Failure taught me resilience. It showed me that every stumble was an opportunity to learn. My shadow tried to use failure to define me, but I fell in love with learning, and I've learned to see it as a step forward, not a step back.

Abandonment is perhaps the deepest fear I carry. The idea of being left behind, whether by loved ones or life itself, has caused me immense pain. My shadow thrives in these moments, amplifying my insecurities and convincing me that I'm not worthy of connection. But through this struggle, I've learned the importance of building a relationship with myself. This is how I began to heal my anxious attachment. I've come to understand that abandonment often reflects wounds from the past, not the reality of the present. By reconnecting with myself and my spiritual source, I've found a sense of wholeness that no one else can take away.

Shame and guilt are emotions I know all too well. They weigh heavily, convincing me that my mistakes define me and that my imperfections make me unworthy. My shadow loves to remind me of every misstep, keeping me trapped in cycles of self-blame and self-sabotage. But as painful as these emotions are, they've shaped me in unexpected ways. They've pushed me to take accountability for my actions and, more importantly, to practice forgiveness, both for myself and others. I've learned that shame is often a mask for a deeper fear: the fear of being truly seen for who I am.

And then there's the fear of loss. Losing people, opportunities, or even parts of myself has been one of the hardest struggles to navigate. My shadow whispers that loss is a punishment or a sign of my failure, but I've come to see it differently. Loss has shaped me by teaching me the value of what I still have. It's shown me how to cherish the present moment and find beauty in impermanence. The shadow may see loss as an ending, but I've learned it's often a beginning, a chance to rebuild and rediscover. A new door.

Through shadow work, I've learned to face my fears with calm and neutrality, a skill I cultivated through the discipline of meditation. In meditation, I trained my eyes—both physical and spiritual—to observe my shadow self without judgment, to simply see what lay beneath the surface. This neutrality became my strength.

By learning to sit with my darkness without reacting, I created a space where I could acknowledge, understand, and analyze it only if I chose to, and only when I chose to. This approach allowed me to step away from the need to fix or fight and instead truly understand the lessons my shadow was presenting. It became clear that my ego often tried to intervene, drawing reactions from fear, pride, or old wounds that I had yet to overcome. Over time, I trained myself to recognize the ego's presence and steer away from it. I practiced identifying when a response was coming from my senses and consciously chose stillness instead.

My mind, however, did not surrender easily. It conjured vivid, holographic-like memories, almost as if testing my resolve. These images were haunting, familiar, and deeply personal, designed to provoke a reaction. But I remained still. I disciplined my mind to observe rather than respond. This wasn't an easy victory—it was a battle I fought repeatedly, each time growing stronger.

My mantra became my shield: "I tell myself what to think. Only *I* tell myself what to believe." These words were my declaration of sovereignty, a reminder that my thoughts belonged to me and me alone. Without them, my mind had the power to lead me down paths of primary and secondary thoughts that weren't my own. I refused to let that happen. I trained myself to be faster than my own thoughts, to intercept them before they could dictate my reality. In doing so, I uncovered a profound truth: limits only exist when we choose to accept them. We see boundaries because we agree to their terms, but when we reject those terms, we step into limitless potential.

This shift in perspective opened me to a deeper connection with the spiritual realm.

One of my first profound encounters came during meditation when a gazelle appeared in my mind's eye. At first, I didn't understand its presence, but curiosity led me to search for its symbolism. The gazelle represents grace, adaptability, and the ability to move through challenges with lightness and ease. In that moment, I realized this wasn't just a random image; it was a spirit guide. The gazelle was there to remind me of the qualities I already possessed but needed to embody more fully. It was showing me how to apply its traits to overcome the specific challenge I was facing.

As a day walker, I've learned to embrace both the light and the dark equally, knowing that pain and fear are not obstacles to avoid but pathways to profound transformation. Walking through the shadows of my own mind, I've discovered that the darkness I once feared holds the very lessons I need to grow. By confronting these truths and transmuting their energy, I've come to see that every struggle and every scar is a step toward wholeness—a reminder of the strength that lies in balance and the grace that comes from walking between worlds.

The Seed in Darkness

There was a time when I felt crushed under the weight of life. It was as though I was buried, unable to see a way out. Everything around me felt dark, heavy, and uncertain. I didn't understand it then, but I wasn't buried, I was planted. The difference is subtle, yet profound. When we are planted, we are placed in the exact conditions needed for transformation. What feels like suffocation and pressure is actually the beginning of something beautiful.

This insight is something I often share with people I care about, especially when they feel surrounded by darkness and pressure. A seed knows nothing of the surface world. Its entire existence is small and contained, unaware of what lies ahead. Then, something shifts. Pressure builds from within, and the protective shell that once held it safe begins to crack. The seed might feel like it's breaking apart, but this breaking is not destruction, it's transformation. In the darkness, the seed begins to change. Its roots stretch down into the soil, seeking stability and nourishment, while its sprout pushes upward, guided by an unseen force toward the light. This transformation is messy and uncertain, but it is the only way for the seed to fulfill its purpose, to become a plant.

In many ways, this mirrors the growth of the lotus flower, which can only bloom because of the mud. Without the

mud—the dark, murky environment filled with nutrients—
the lotus could not root itself, grow, or emerge into the
sunlight. This idea of "no mud, no lotus" has profoundly
shaped how I understand discomfort. Like the lotus, we must
embrace the challenges and uncertainties of life because they
provide the foundation for our growth. The mud of life, the
struggles, setbacks, and pain, feeds us in ways we don't always
understand, helping us become stronger, more resilient, and
more connected to who we are meant to be. Learning to
accept this truth has allowed me to maintain a more neutral
background when navigating the complexities of life as a Day
Walker—someone who walks the line between extremes,
finding balance in light and dark. The discomfort and
pressure I've faced are not enemies to avoid, but teachers to
learn from. The seed does not resist the soil, and the lotus
does not reject the mud. Instead, they use these elements to
transform, grow, and thrive.

In life, this same breaking and pushing happens to us. Under
stress, pain, or uncertainty, we feel like we're falling apart. But
that breaking is the first step toward growth. Even after
breaking, the sprout doesn't have it easy. It must push
through the soil, inch by inch, in a blind search for light.
Every moment is a struggle. The soil is heavy, and the sprout
is delicate, yet it keeps pushing.

Why? Because growth is instinctual, and light is its purpose. As humans, we experience this too. After the initial breaking, we face resistance at every turn. The weight of doubt, fear, and discomfort can feel unbearable. Yet, like the sprout, we are designed to grow. While we can't always see the light, we must trust that it is there, waiting for us. I remind people that even when they feel like they are breaking under the pressure, it's not the end, it's the beginning of something new.

Growth often feels like death because, in many ways, it is. To grow, we must let go of what no longer serves us, old identities, beliefs, or habits. It's a process of shedding and renewal, and it's rarely comfortable. I tell my loved ones that when they feel like they're dying from stress, it's often a sign that something old is ending to make way for something new. The stress is the labor of rebirth. Think of diamonds, formed under unimaginable pressure, or fine wine, perfected only through time. Growth is the same. It is forged in discomfort and polished by patience.

The pressure you feel is not an ending, but a beginning. If you feel like you're breaking, it's because you are, but not in the way you fear. You're breaking open, making room for something extraordinary to emerge. You are not buried. You are planted. The darkness you feel is the starting point of your transformation, and the pressure you're under is shaping you into something extraordinary.

Trust the process. Push through the soil. The light is waiting for you, and when you find it, you'll realize the darkness was not your enemy—it was your catalyst.

Chapter 3 Shadow Work

When I first began exploring my shadow, I quickly realized that self-compassion wasn't just helpful—it was fundamental. Shadow Work isn't merely about identifying the parts of myself I've hidden or denied; it's about meeting them with kindness, understanding, and patience. Without compassion as my guide, I would have been left wrestling with overwhelming emotions: guilt for the things I hadn't dealt with, shame for the parts of me I didn't want to see, and fear of what this process might reveal. Self-compassion became the bridge between self-awareness and self-acceptance, and without it, I don't know if I could have continued.

I found myself standing before the abyss, ready to plunge into its depths. I knew if I wasn't cautious, I could exacerbate my situation. With a commitment to confront every shadow within me, I aimed to bring light to the darkness. Though the duration of this journey remained uncertain, my determination to heal and overcome my challenges was unwavering, and it was decided—there was no stopping me.

Facing my shadow wasn't a neat or comfortable process; it was raw, messy, and often vulnerable in ways I hadn't anticipated. It was usually intimidating and felt counterintuitive. Confronting buried fears, ingrained beliefs, and old wounds was deeply uncomfortable, and at times, I felt utterly exposed, even to myself—like being made of glass, fragile and see-through. But that's when self-compassion became my safe haven. Instead of running from what I found, I practiced sitting with it, breathing through the discomfort, and reminding myself that these parts of me existed for a reason. They were products of my experiences, my defenses, and my unmet needs, and they deserved to be seen, not hidden away. Self-compassion helped me create a space where my shadow could exist without judgment, a space where healing could begin.

Shame was one of the heaviest emotions I encountered during Shadow Work. It would creep in like an unwelcome guest, whispering that there was something fundamentally wrong with me because of what I'd repressed or avoided. There were moments when I felt like I was drowning in it, questioning if I was even worthy of the growth I sought. It was too easy to fall apart and crumble. I learned that shame doesn't have to define me. Self-compassion gave me a way to soften its grip, to look at my shadow and say, "I see you. I understand why you're here. And I choose to meet you with love." Embracing this perspective taught me that my shadow isn't a reflection of my failures; it's a reflection of my humanity.

Healing didn't come instantly, and it wasn't linear. It came in layers, and each layer required a willingness to forgive myself. Forgiving myself wasn't about ignoring the ways I'd fallen short or excusing harmful behaviors; it was about recognizing that those actions were often born from wounds and unmet needs I hadn't yet healed. I followed a mantra: "I know I could not have acted in a more evolved way than I was able to at the time." Self-compassion allowed me to approach those patterns with curiosity rather than condemnation. It became clear that true healing doesn't happen through rejection; it happens through integration. When I welcomed these disowned parts of myself back into the fold, I experienced a sense of wholeness that had always felt out of reach.

There were times when the process felt unbearable, oppressive, and torturous. The weight of old emotions and the sheer magnitude of what I was uncovering made me want to quit. In those moments, I leaned into self-compassion and grounding, not as an escape but as a source of strength. Compassion reminded me that I didn't have to do it all at once, that it was okay to take breaks, to rest, and to move forward at my own pace. It taught me that courage doesn't mean being fearless; it means staying present even when it hurts, trusting that the discomfort will pass and that I'm capable of holding it. This resilience, nurtured by compassion, allowed me to face emotions I once thought would destroy me.

Through this practice, I've learned to accept myself in ways I never thought possible. I've stopped waging war against the parts of me I don't like and have instead chosen to embrace all of me—my light and my shadow, my strengths and my struggles. As I moved deeper into this journey, I began to focus on a simple mantra I lived by during the intensity of this process: "Never again will I wage war against myself." These words became a grounding force, a reminder that my shadow is not my enemy but a part of me seeking acknowledgment and healing. It was an affirmation.

This wasn't just about healing old wounds; it was about integrating every part of my being into a cohesive whole. The parts of me I once feared or rejected didn't disappear; they transformed. By holding them with self-compassion, I transmuted their energy from something that felt heavy and limiting into a source of wisdom and strength. What once felt like chaos became clarity; what once felt like conflict became balance.

And so, I now carry this understanding forward: the parts of me I once tried to hide were never broken or wrong. They were calling out for my attention, my kindness, and my willingness to see them for what they truly are. By embracing them, I've become more than just whole—I've become aligned. This is the power of Shadow Work, and this is why self-compassion is its most essential ingredient. It is what transforms the journey from one of struggle into one of empowerment, from fragmentation into unity, from shadow into light.

Grounding: Holding Myself Steady in the Dark

Shadow work isn't just about uncovering what's hidden—it's about learning how to hold myself through it. There are moments when I feel like I'm sinking, when emotions rise like waves that threaten to pull me under. My emotions quickly shift to quicksand, becoming an undertow that I'm lost in. That's why I ground myself. It's my anchor, my way of staying present while facing what needs to be seen.

At first, I didn't think much about grounding. It felt abstract, like something that belonged in meditation circles or spiritual practices outside my reach—foreign and complicated to grasp. But Shai, a deep friend, and my shaman, Shaman Om, through his wisdom, helped me see that grounding isn't just a concept; it's survival. It's how I steady myself when stress presses in from all sides, how I make it through triggers without losing myself to them. It's not just something I do when I sit down with intention; it's something I rely on throughout my day, in the small, unseen moments no one else witnesses.

In the morning, before I even open my eyes, I feel my body against the sheets—the weight of the blanket, the warmth of my skin, the sound of my own breath. I used to roll out of bed and immediately get lost in the whirlwind of responsibilities, but now I take a few seconds to just be. I remind myself that I am here, that this is a new day, and that I am allowed to move through it at my own pace. I set my intentions and recite affirmations.

Some days, I don't get much time before stress starts creeping in. Maybe it's an unexpected message that tightens my chest, a reminder of something I wish I could forget, or just that familiar heaviness that sometimes follows me for no reason at all. At times, I wake up feeling in between realms. I feel it before I have time to think about it—my stomach knots, my breath shortens, my mind starts spinning stories I don't want to hear. This is where grounding saves me.

I pause, even if I'm mid-movement, even if I'm in the middle of a conversation. I find something to bring me back. I touch the fabric of my sleeve, rub my thumb against the inside of my wrist, or press my feet firmly to the floor. Sometimes, I whisper to myself—not out loud, but just beneath the surface of thought: *I am here. I am safe.* If I have a few extra seconds, I breathe deeper. I let the air stretch my lungs, let my exhales be longer than my inhales, and let my nervous system catch up to the truth that I am not in danger.

On harder days, when stress doesn't just knock but pushes its way in, I turn to something more physical. I step outside, even if just for a minute. I feel the air on my skin, let my fingers graze a leaf or a patch of grass, and let the earth remind me that I am part of something bigger than my pain. If stepping outside isn't an option, I hold onto a stone or a crystal—something cool and solid in my palm, something real. I remind myself that no matter what's happening inside my head, the world is still here. I am still here.

At night, when thoughts feel the loudest, grounding is what keeps me from spiraling. I used to fight sleep, restless in my own body, but now I give myself something gentle to hold onto. Sometimes, it's the rhythm of my breath. Sometimes, it's the sound of healing frequencies playing softly in the background. Other times, it's simply the reminder that I made it through another day, that I don't have to figure everything out before I close my eyes.

Grounding is how I get through the heaviness. It's how I

remind myself that I am more than my past, more than my pain, more than whatever weight I am carrying in the moment. It's not a magic fix. Some days, it takes effort. Some days, I forget and find myself untethered, floating too far into my thoughts before I even realize it. But the beauty of grounding is that I can return at any moment. I don't have to be perfect. I just have to be here. And that is enough.

Recognizing and Befriending My Shadow

I used to seriously believe my shadow was something to fight against—something ugly, something dangerous, something that needed to be tamed. The more I resisted it, the more it showed up in ways I couldn't control. I would find myself reacting too intensely to situations, getting stuck in patterns I thought I had already outgrown.

I saw my wounds reflected in the way I spoke to myself, in the fears that kept me small, and in the moments when I felt unworthy of love. It took me a long time to realize that my shadow wasn't trying to harm me. It wasn't a monster lurking in the dark; it was simply the part of me I had abandoned— the parts I was told were too much, too messy, too shameful.

My shadow was my pain, my rage, my unmet needs, my hidden desires, and my mistakes, all waiting to be acknowledged. The moment I stopped running from it and turned toward it with curiosity, I felt something shift. My shadow wasn't something to defeat; it was a piece of me longing to be understood.

Now, I try to meet my shadow with the same compassion I would offer to a wounded child. When I notice patterns repeating or emotions rising unexpectedly, I don't judge myself as harshly as I once did. Instead, I ask: *What are you trying to tell me?* Slowly, my shadow reveals itself—not as something separate from me, but as an integral part of who I am.

Unpacking My Core Wounds and Triggers

There was a time when I believed my emotions controlled me. I would feel anger, sadness, or jealousy bubble up, and I would either suppress them or let them take over completely. I never stopped to ask why these emotions were surfacing in the first place.

But I've learned that every trigger is a messenger, pointing to something unresolved within me. When something stings, when someone's words cut deeper than they should, or when a situation makes me feel small, I pause. Instead of reacting impulsively, I ask myself: *Where have I felt this before?*

Sometimes, the answer takes me back to childhood, to moments when I felt unheard, unseen, or unworthy. Other times, the pain doesn't feel entirely mine, as if I'm carrying echoes of wounds passed down through my lineage or absorbing rather than observing as an empath.

This work is difficult but necessary. It's not about blaming the past; it's about understanding it so I don't continue to repeat the same cycles. By tracing my emotions to their roots, I gain the power to choose a different response. I remind myself that I am no longer that child seeking validation, nor am I bound by the patterns of those who came before me. I have the power to rewrite my own story.

Shadow work is not always easy. There are moments when I want to turn away, when I tell myself I don't have time for this, or when I convince myself that I'm fine. I recognize this for what it is: resistance. My ego has done a good job of protecting me, shielding me from pain I wasn't ready to process. It built walls around my wounds so I wouldn't have to feel them.

But now, those same walls are keeping me from growing. I've come to understand that my resistance is not a sign of failure; it's a sign that I'm stepping into something unfamiliar, something vulnerable. Instead of forcing my way through, I practice gentleness. I acknowledge my fears without letting them dictate my path. When my mind tells me to avoid something, I ask: *What am I afraid to see?* If an emotion feels overwhelming, I take a breath and remind myself that I don't have to rush. Healing is not a race; it's a journey.

Embracing My Darkness and Light

For so long, I saw shadow work as a way to purge the "bad" parts of me. I thought if I did enough inner work, I would finally be free of anger, sadness, jealousy, and insecurity—all the emotions I deemed unworthy of being seen. But I was wrong. Shadow work wasn't about erasing parts of myself; it has been about embracing all of me.

I've learned that my darkness is not separate from my light. They exist together, intertwined, each giving depth to the other. The same intensity that fuels my anger also fuels my passion. The depth of my sorrow is the same depth that allows me to love so fiercely. My ability to feel deeply, even when it hurts, is a strength, not a weakness.

Instead of fighting against my emotions, I hold space for them. I remind myself that there is nothing wrong with feeling, nothing wrong with being human. My shadow is not something to fix—it is something to integrate. The more I allow all parts of myself to exist without shame, the more whole I become.

Shadow work is not just something I think about; it's something I embody. Some days, I write letters to the parts of myself I have ignored, giving them the voice they never had. Other days, I sit in front of the mirror and hold my own gaze, whispering words of acceptance to the reflection staring back at me. When emotions feel too heavy, I turn to my breath, letting it guide me through the places in my body where I feel tension.

I also remind myself that I don't have to hold everything alone. I work with symbols and energies that resonate with me—sometimes Thoth, guiding me with wisdom; sometimes Anubis, walking me through transformation. These archetypes remind me that shadow work is sacred, that there is power in the darkness just as there is in the light.

I have learned that healing is not about perfection. It is not about reaching a point where I never struggle again. It is about being present with myself, accepting myself in every stage of my journey. My shadow is not my enemy; it is my teacher. Every time I meet it with love instead of fear, I take another step toward becoming who I am meant to be.

Chapter 4 Awakening to the Light

What is the Light? Discovering Spiritual Light: A Personal Journey

There is a light within you, always has been, always will be. Even in the moments when life feels heavy, when the shadows seem to close in, that light remains. It doesn't demand perfection from you or wait for the "right" moment to appear. It's there, quietly offering itself, ready for you to notice it.

Spiritual light isn't about reaching a finish line or becoming someone new. It's about learning to embrace three powerful forces: love, wisdom, and purpose. These aren't abstract ideas or impossible ideals. They're already a part of you, waiting to be felt in your own way, in your own time.

Of course, love is where it all begins. It's the spark that connects us all—to ourselves, to each other, and to the world. Maybe love feels far away right now; that's okay. Love doesn't have to come in grand gestures. It can be an act as simple as offering yourself a kind word after a long day or choosing to see someone else with compassionate eyes, even when it's hard. Think of the moments when you've felt warmth or care, no matter how small. That's love. It's a gentle reminder that you're never truly alone. If love feels impossible today, know that it's patient and on its way, showing you it has always been silently waiting to be heard.

Wisdom is the light that guides you forward, even when the path ahead feels unclear. It's not about knowing everything or making perfect choices. It's a profound understanding that emerges from connecting with universal truths and higher consciousness. It transcends intellectual knowledge, allowing us to grasp deeper meanings of life. Wisdom lives in the quiet places within us, in the moments when we trust our instincts or when we learn from our experiences. Maybe you've felt it before, like a nudge toward something that felt right, even if you couldn't explain why. Or maybe it's the realization that even the hardest days have taught you something valuable. Wisdom isn't loud or demanding; it whispers about embracing growth and learning from each moment.

And then there's purpose—the unique reason we're here. It's not about achieving greatness in the eyes of the world. Success appears differently for everyone. Your purpose doesn't have to be big or flashy. It might be found in the way you care for others, in the creativity you bring to life, or in the quiet moments where you simply show up as yourself. It's all connected; we're all connected. Purpose doesn't ask you to have everything figured out. It grows with you, revealing itself in small, meaningful ways. If you're still searching, that's okay. Every step, even the uncertain ones, is part of discovering it.

These three—love, wisdom, and purpose—are the threads of spiritual light, weaving through every moment of your life. Some days, they might feel bright and easy to notice. Other days, they might feel distant or even unreachable. Don't be discouraged; that's part of being human. Healing isn't a straight line, and there's no rush to "get there." Wherever you are in your journey, you're already enough. The fact that you're here, reading this, searching for meaning, is proof of the light within you.

It's okay to take small steps. It's okay to feel stuck sometimes. The light doesn't judge. It simply waits, patiently, for you to notice it again, no matter how often you question its whereabouts. There's a whole world of others walking their own paths, carrying their own shadows and light. Together, we learn, we grow, and we heal. And that's why we're all here—not to rush toward perfection, but to rediscover the light within us, to embrace it, and to share it in ways only we can. In doing so, we illuminate not just our own path but the paths of others, reminding them—and ourselves—that the light was never lost. It was always here, waiting to be seen.

Awakening, whether spiritual or personal, has led me to experience profound shifts in perspective that have significantly impacted various aspects of my life. It began with heightened awareness, allowing me to gain a deeper understanding of my thoughts, emotions, and behaviors, revealing patterns I had previously overlooked. This journey has fostered a stronger sense of connection to others and the universe, enhancing my empathy and compassion in relationships.

As I continued to awaken, I reassessed my values, prioritizing relationships, experiences, and personal growth over material possessions and societal expectations. Letting go of my ego has been a crucial part of my awakening journey, though it's not about eliminating it entirely. Instead, I've learned to recognize its limitations and how it shapes my identity and interactions with the world.

Initially, my sense of self was tightly bound to external validations, achievements, and the opinions of others. As I've explored this process, I've experienced a profound liberation that allows me to see myself and others more clearly. I've started to understand that I am not merely my thoughts, emotions, or experiences, but something far greater—an ever-evolving being in a vast and interconnected universe. This awareness helps me maintain a balance between my feelings and the world around me, allowing me to embrace my role as a Day Walker.

This shift has also changed how I view challenges and adversities. Rather than seeing them as roadblocks or sources of suffering, I now embrace them as invaluable opportunities for growth and learning while thinking of them as tools for growth and ultimately—transformation. Each challenge presents a lesson, nudging me toward greater resilience and self-discovery. This perspective fosters a more positive outlook, transforming my response to difficult situations into a proactive search for insight and understanding, something I now prioritize after understanding the crucial aspect it holds.

Moreover, I've begun to recognize the beauty of vulnerability that comes with this journey. I'm learning to express my true feelings and share my authentic self with others, cultivating deeper connections that transcend superficial interactions. Navigating this process of letting go of the ego requires constant reflection and commitment, and while I haven't completely released it, I find a balance that allows me to embrace my authentic self while still engaging with the world. This ongoing journey is deeply rewarding, providing me with a sense of peace and clarity that pervades every aspect of my life.

As I continue to explore this path, I feel increasingly empowered to navigate life's complexities with grace and confidence. Ultimately, this understanding of my ego has opened up new horizons for personal growth and connection, deepening my understanding of who I am and my place in the world.

As I continue to awaken, I've also found myself re-evaluating long-held beliefs, becoming more open to new ideas and possibilities, which has promoted a more expansive worldview. The more I learn and overcome, the more I accept, the more I gain. Present-moment awareness has become a vital aspect of my life, allowing me to appreciate the beauty of life as it unfolds instead of being caught up in regrets about the past or worries about the future. Integrating spiritual practices, such as meditation and mindfulness, into my daily routine has further enhanced my understanding and perspective.

Finally, this awakened mindset has helped me embrace the transient nature of existence, nurturing acceptance and appreciation for each moment rather than fear of loss or change. This transformative journey continues to enrich my experience of life, leading to deeper connections, insights, and a more profound sense of purpose.

Living in alignment in spiritual terms is a profound, ongoing journey of harmonizing my inner world—my thoughts, actions, values, and beliefs—with my higher self and divine purpose. This path invites me to continuously reflect, adjust, and grow as I strive to embody my most authentic and elevated self.

At its core, alignment begins with a commitment to authenticity, where I consciously choose to honor the truth of who I am over the comfort of societal conformity. For example, if I feel a profound connection to nature, I may prioritize experiences that deepen this bond, such as hiking through serene landscapes, meditating by the ocean, or simply observing the gentle rhythm of the natural world. Sometimes, when I go for a walk, I take time to observe the ducks. I watch them with neutrality, embracing their energy and the purpose they embody, knowing all things are connected. I do the same with trees, though it's hard to focus on each one as I pass. I listen to the streams; the sound of moving water fills my senses, its energy washing over me, clearing and renewing my own. In doing so, I allow this connection to nourish my spirit, grounding me in the beauty of existence and reminding me of the interconnectedness of life.

As I explore my life's purpose, I feel a deep sense of joy and fulfillment when pursuing passions that resonate with the essence of my soul. Whether it's creating art that channels my inner emotions or sharing knowledge that uplifts others, each action becomes a sacred expression of my purpose.

Mindfulness is a cornerstone of this journey, encouraging me to remain fully present and aware of my internal and external experiences. This heightened awareness empowers me to make intentional choices that reflect my core values and spiritual aspirations. For instance, when facing a challenging decision, I might pause to meditate or journal, connecting with my intuition to ensure my choice aligns with my higher truth.

Anchoring my life in values such as compassion, love, honesty, and integrity forms a foundation that nurtures my spiritual growth. I practice these values in both subtle and profound ways by extending kindness to others, offering a listening ear, or holding space for someone in need. These small but meaningful actions create ripples of positivity that align with the greater good.

Trusting my intuition becomes an essential guide, illuminating my path with clarity and confidence. When I feel drawn to a new opportunity, relationship, or community, I embrace it with faith, understanding that my inner guidance is attuned to my spiritual evolution. Trusting my intuition has been a journey of growth and adjustment. In the beginning, it wasn't easy. I had to distinguish its voice from the noise of doubt and fear. Over time, I came to understand that my higher self and divine forces were always present, guiding me even through the darkest chapters of my healing.

I realized that the frequency I operate in deeply influences my connection to intuition. When my energy is aligned and elevated, my intuition becomes clearer and stronger. As I've worked to strengthen its voice, I've discovered that trust is the foundation of it all—trust in myself, in the guidance I receive, and in the process of unfolding that's beyond my control. This trust has become the cornerstone of my growth, helping me embrace my intuition not as something separate, but as an integral part of who I am. This trust fosters a sense of flow, where life unfolds in harmony with my true essence.

Recognizing my connection to all beings and the universe deepens my sense of unity and compassion. It reminds me of the profound relationship we share with the world around us. Recognizing this connection enables me to view everything with neutral eyes, free from bias and preconceived notions. Regardless of what presents itself before me, I can disengage from automatic thoughts and discard them, allowing me to hold space for my observations without judgment. This approach embraces the opportunity to learn and evolve, fostering personal growth and deeper understanding.

I celebrate the shared humanity that binds us, approaching others with empathy and understanding in the face of differences. This interconnected perspective allows me to view challenges not as isolating struggles but as shared opportunities for growth and transformation. Every experience, whether joyous or challenging, becomes a teacher on this path of alignment.

Setbacks are no longer viewed as failures but as sacred opportunities to reflect, adapt, and evolve. For instance, moments of hardship encourage me to cultivate resilience and self-awareness, unlocking deeper layers of wisdom within me. Striving for balance across all dimensions of my being—physical, emotional, mental, and spiritual—becomes a sacred practice that enhances inner peace and harmony. I might dedicate time to nurturing myself through activities such as yoga, journaling, using my shamanic drum, or connecting with loved ones, creating space to recharge and realign.

Ultimately, living in alignment is a continuous, intentional practice of acting in harmony with my soul's purpose. It is a beautiful dance of self-discovery, growth, and connection—a journey where every step reflects the essence of my truth, filling my life with meaning, fulfillment, and divine grace.

The Dance of Awakening

Spiritual awakening didn't arrive like a single revelation. It unfolded slowly, layer by layer, shifting my perspective in ways I never expected. It was like stepping out of a narrow, dimly lit room into an open landscape filled with light and endless depth. At first, I resisted, clinging to the familiarity of my old perceptions, but once the cracks formed, there was no going back. They say a mind cannot return to its old dimensions once it has been stretched beyond them. I agree. Every belief I had once held tightly began to loosen, revealing a world that had always been there but had waited for me to truly see it.

The first thing that changed was the way I saw myself. I had spent so much time identifying with my past, my struggles, my triumphs, the roles I played for others, especially unresolved pain. I thought that was my identity. I was my name, my experiences, my wounds, my expectations. But as I woke up, I realized that these were only fragments of something much larger. Those details were just details. The "I" I had always known was just a construct, a fleeting identity shaped by conditioning, memories, and fears. Beneath it, there was something deeper—something boundless, connected, and eternal. I was no longer just a person moving through the world; I was the world, and the world was me. There was no separation.

With this shift, my awareness expanded in ways I could never have imagined. It wasn't just about noticing more; it was about seeing and behaving differently, like being granted a new set of eyes—multiple sets of eyes, inherently. The world became more vibrant, more alive. Patterns emerged where I once saw chaos. Synchronicities became impossible to dismiss. The way the wind carried whispers through the trees, the way strangers' lives briefly intersected with mine at just the right moments, the way my thoughts and emotions seemed to ripple out and return in unexpected ways—it all spoke of an intricate design that had been invisible to me before. Even rush hour traffic became a fractal symphonic pattern resembling arterial dynamics. I began to feel the energy behind words, sensing the unspoken emotions people carried, understanding that silence sometimes held more truth than speech. I was becoming one with existence.

The things I used to chase began to lose their meaning. Success, validation, material comfort—I had spent so much time reaching for things outside of myself, believing they would fill the spaces within. But as I woke up, I realized that these pursuits had only kept me distracted from the truth. What once seemed urgent now felt insignificant. I no longer measured my worth by achievements or the approval of others. Instead, I found value in stillness, in depth, in simply existing with awareness. My priorities shifted without effort. I stopped searching for meaning in the external and started uncovering it within. So, as they say, "the only way out is through." And so it is.

Along with this came a softening of the way I viewed others. Judgment, once so reflexive, began to dissolve. I realized that understanding is the answer to disengage in common situations, the missing link. I could no longer feel as mad; it wasn't the same anymore, nothing was, not after truth was discovered. I saw that everyone carried their own burdens, their own unhealed wounds, their own moments of awakening and resistance. I stopped placing people into categories of "good" or "bad," realizing that we are all navigating this existence with the awareness available to us at any given moment. I learned that forgiveness wasn't about excusing harm but about freeing myself from the chains of resentment. The more I understood my own struggles, the more I understood others, and in that understanding, compassion replaced division. We are all on the same journey; the only difference is the stage and the self-awareness achieved.

Fear, which had once held me captive, also began to lose its power. The unknown, which used to terrify me, became something I could sit with, even welcome. I no longer feared loss the way I once did, because I understood that nothing was ever truly lost, only transformed. I stopped dreading endings, knowing they were merely transitions into new beginnings. Like Yin and Yang, creation and destruction go hand in hand. Pain, and even suffering, held lessons that I could no longer ignore. Everything became a tool. I began to trust in life's unfolding, even when I couldn't see where it was leading me. There was a deep knowing that everything, even the struggles, was part of something greater. Everything was truly connected.

The world no longer felt divided into absolutes. I used to see life in rigid contrasts—right and wrong, light and dark, good and evil. But the more I awakened, the more these dualities blurred. I saw that darkness was not the absence of light but a necessary part of it. That pain and joy were not opposites, but companions. That destruction often paved the way for rebirth. Nothing was singular; everything existed in balance, in cycles, in a dance of contrasts that I had once misunderstood as opposition. And so I learned to dance to the rhythm of creation, dancing between worlds, learning and unleashing, one symphony at a time.

My intuition, once a quiet whisper, became a guiding force. I stopped doubting the subtle nudges, the inner knowing, the dreams that felt like messages. Logic was no longer my only compass. There was something beyond it, something that could not be measured or explained, yet felt undeniably real. I started listening. I started following. And the more I trusted, the more life seemed to flow effortlessly, aligning in ways I could never have orchestrated on my own. The more I followed, the more I witnessed, the more I truly lived.

Even time itself felt different. I spent less energy reliving the past or anxiously reaching for the future. Instead, I found myself more present, more in tune with the moment I was in. There were times when time seemed to dissolve completely, when I existed purely in the now, where life wasn't something happening to me but through me. I found Zen. These moments felt like eternity and an instant all at once, as if I had stepped beyond the confines of time and into something infinite.

This journey has not been easy. Awakening is not a gentle unfolding; it is a breaking, a dismantling of everything I once believed to be true. It is seeing the beauty in chaos. There have been moments of profound loneliness, of disorientation, of grieving the self I once was. But despite the discomfort, despite the shedding, I could never go back. The illusion has been lifted. And now, all I can do is keep walking forward, keep expanding, keep surrendering to the truth that has always been waiting for me to see it.

Chapter 5 Identifying and Honoring Your Soul

There comes a moment when we begin to wonder if we're truly living in alignment with who we are. It's not always a loud realization. Sometimes, it's a quiet knowing, an intuitive feeling that something more is calling us. The journey to uncovering our soul path isn't about following a strict set of rules or striving to meet external expectations. Instead, it's about listening, allowing, and embracing the uniqueness of your path, knowing that no one else can walk it but you. It's a personal journey of self-discovery.

Living in alignment means honoring what feels true at your core, not what the world tells you should be true. It's about peeling back the layers of conditioning, fear, and doubt to remember who you are beneath it all—the part of yourself without what you needed to become to get this far. And the truth is, your soul path was never meant to fit into a predefined mold; it was meant to be discovered, shaped, and lived in a way that is entirely your own.

But how do you begin to recognize it? How do you know if you're walking in alignment with your soul's calling? This journey isn't about rushing to find answers—if it were, there wouldn't be a destination. It's about learning to ask the right questions, paying attention to the quiet whispers of intuition, and trusting that every step, even the uncertain ones, is part of your unfolding story.

It starts with reflection—not the kind that demands answers, but the kind that invites curiosity. What makes you lose track of time? What moments in life have felt the most real, the most alive? When you let your mind wander without boundaries, where does it take you? Do you question it? Do you believe all your thoughts? The root of your thoughts— are they yours or echoes of poor coping mechanisms and conditioning? These questions aren't meant to be solved in a day but explored over time, like a slow unraveling of truth. Journaling can be a beautiful way to capture these thoughts, but even if all you do is sit in quiet contemplation, you're already opening the door to understanding yourself in a deeper way.

In a world filled with noise, finding moments of stillness can feel like a luxury. But within that stillness, answers emerge— not always as words, but as feelings, visions, or a deep sense of knowing. Meditation, visualization, or simply breathing with intention can help you connect with what lies beneath the surface. Picture your life without limitations—what does it look like? What impact do you hope to leave behind? The images that arise aren't random; they're glimpses into what your soul longs for, an internal compass.

Sometimes, alignment feels like a gentle pull toward something that excites you, even if you can't explain why. It's the sudden spark when you talk about a certain topic, the unshakable feeling that something is meant for you. Pay attention to those moments. Your intuition speaks in whispers, in sensations, in quiet nudges that urge you forward. The more you trust it, the more it reveals. If you look back at your life, you might notice recurring themes—passions that never faded, lessons that kept reappearing, or dreams that refused to be forgotten. These patterns are not coincidences; they are signposts. What have you always been drawn to? What activities bring you a deep sense of fulfillment? Your purpose is often woven into the things that light you up. It's what makes you who you are.

Every experience, whether joyful or painful, has shaped you in some way. The moments that broke you, the ones that lifted you, the choices that led you here—all of it carries wisdom. Your soul path isn't just about what excites you; it's also about what you've learned. What have your struggles taught you? What insights have emerged from the difficult seasons of your life? Within those answers lies a deeper understanding of where you are meant to go. Your soul path isn't about becoming someone else; it's about embracing who you already are.

Tools like personality assessments can offer insight, but the real wisdom comes from within. You are not here to fit into a mold; you are here to embody your truth. The more you lean into your natural strengths and inclinations, the clearer your path becomes. Once you begin to see the shape of your path, even if only faintly, setting intentions can help bring it into focus—not in a way that pressures or confines you, but in a way that serves as a gentle reminder of what you're moving toward. A vision board, affirmations, or even a simple statement of purpose can act as anchors, keeping you aligned with what feels true to you. It's a lifestyle of moving forward.

The environment we create, both physically and emotionally, plays a big role in how we align with our path. Does your space feel like a reflection of yourself or the people in your journey? Are the people around you supportive of your growth, or do they hinder you? Small changes, like clearing out what no longer serves you or surrounding yourself with those who uplift you, can create a foundation that nurtures your journey, even if you are your own circle. It's important to surround yourself with an environment that offers support—not just the people in your life, but everything you do yourself.

Every day, we make countless decisions, big and small. Before saying yes to something, pause and ask yourself: Does this resonate with who I am or who I want to be? Sometimes, the simplest questions bring the clearest answers. Living in alignment isn't about making perfect choices; it's about making conscious ones, ones that feel right in your heart, even if they don't make sense to everyone else.

Honoring your soul path also means taking care of the vessel that carries you through it. What restores you? What quiets the noise and brings you back to yourself? Whether it's spending time in nature, creating, being still, or movement like yoga or dancing to your favorite songs, self-care isn't just a luxury—it's a way to stay connected to your truth.

Your path is not a straight line, nor is it meant to be. It twists, it shifts, it expands—it's alive. What feels aligned today may evolve tomorrow, and that's okay. Be open to change, to new directions, to the unfolding of your journey in ways you didn't expect. Growth is part of the process, and alignment isn't about reaching a final destination; it's about continuing to walk with awareness and trust. It's about the journey.

At the core of it all is authenticity—the courage to be who you are, fully and unapologetically. When you live in alignment with your soul path, life moves differently. Opportunities appear, connections deepen, and there is a sense of ease, even in the challenges. It doesn't mean everything is perfect, but it means you are at peace with the direction you're heading and with who you are.

There is no finish line to this work. There is only the unfolding, the becoming, the continuous dance of discovering who you are and what you are here to do. Celebrate the small moments, the shifts in awareness, the steps forward. Every insight, every realization, every choice that aligns you with your truth is worth honoring. Living in alignment isn't about perfection. It's about presence, about listening, about allowing yourself to be guided by what feels real and true. It's a journey meant just for you, unfolding in its own time, in its own way. And as you walk it, you will find that the more you honor your soul path, the more life opens itself to you in ways you never imagined.

Cultivating Gratitude, Mindfulness, and Presence

As I strive to stay in alignment with my true self, I have discovered several key factors that nurture this harmony, with raising my frequency being paramount. Gratitude has emerged as one of the simplest yet most profound ways to elevate my spirit and transition my mind into a state of balance and peace. It serves as a gateway, opening the door to a brighter perspective. Alongside this, mindfulness has played a crucial role in my journey. Through the lens of Zen poetry, I learned the beauty of being present, which has been instrumental in preventing my mind from spiraling when stress lurked nearby. The powerful combination of gratitude and mindfulness helped me navigate through some of my darkest moments, igniting a deep desire within me to share these practices with others, guiding them toward their own paths of healing and alignment.

To embrace gratitude in your life, consider starting a daily gratitude journaling practice. Each day, set aside a few moments to pause and reflect on the things that fill your heart with appreciation. This can be as simple as a warm cup of tea or the laughter of a loved one. When it comes to gratitude, nothing is too small. Imagine waking up with only the things you're grateful for. Now, I hope you realize it's about not taking things for granted and instead finding balance through the simple, small things that connect everything in our lives. By writing down three things you are grateful for, you allow yourself to savor these moments, letting the warmth of gratitude envelop you.

Another meaningful way to express gratitude is through letters. Reach out to someone who has positively impacted your life and write them a heartfelt letter. Sharing your appreciation can bring joy not only to you but also to the recipient. Additionally, take moments throughout your day to practice mindful appreciation. When you feel the sun on your skin or taste your favorite food, breathe deeply and let gratitude wash over you like a gentle wave.

Mindfulness invites us to be fully present, embracing each moment without judgment. A wonderful practice to begin with is mindful breathing. Find a comfortable space, close your eyes, and take a deep breath in, feeling the air fill your lungs before slowly exhaling. Repeat this several times, allowing your breath to anchor you in the present and letting your worries drift away. You might also try a body scan meditation, where you connect with your body by slowly bringing awareness to each part, starting from your toes and moving up. This practice fosters self-awareness and helps ground you.

As you cultivate mindfulness, choose an object—a flower, a stone, or even a simple piece of fruit—and spend a few minutes observing it closely. Notice its colors, textures, and shapes, engaging your senses fully. It's okay for this process to take several practices. It's a lifestyle; the vision is to start and not stop. Slow progress is better than no progress. Nurturing presence means allowing ourselves to experience each moment fully. When you eat, savor each bite, focusing on the flavors and sensations. Put away distractions and truly connect with your meal, letting gratitude fill your heart.

Consider taking a digital detox to create space for deeper connections with yourself and your surroundings. Unplugging for a while can lead to meaningful moments, whether that's spending an evening reading a book or enjoying a long bath. Step outside and immerse yourself in nature's beauty. Whether you take a stroll in the park or sit quietly in your backyard, breathe in the fresh air and let the sights and sounds ground you in the present. Whatever the activity, the goal is to enjoy that moment and that moment alone.

Something that helped me understand this in more depth was an act of holding my breath. Inhale deeply, hold it. Hold your breath for as long as you can while paying attention to your thoughts fading as you become aware of what now matters most—the need to exhale. I held my breath until my mind went silent. This helped me understand how loud my mind truly was. Whenever I practiced mindfulness, at first, I focused on the feeling I achieved and reminded myself to reach for the quiet moment that can be found when you hold your breath. Over time, I was able to achieve this state of mind without the act of holding my breath.

As you explore these practices, you may notice how they intertwine beautifully. Start your meditation with a moment of gratitude or express appreciation for the beauty of nature during your walks. Allow these practices to support one another, enriching your experience of life. After trying these practices, take time to reflect on how they made you feel. Consider keeping a journal to capture your thoughts and feelings, noting any shifts you notice within yourself.

Be gentle with your progress, recognizing that integrating these practices into your daily routine doesn't have to be overwhelming. Start small and let them grow naturally, embracing the journey as a beautiful part of your story. Open your heart to the beauty of life, slow down, breathe deeply, and appreciate the moments that make your life uniquely yours.

Chapter 6 Becoming a Lightworker

I've come to understand that being a channel means serving as a bridge between higher spiritual realms and the physical world. As a lightworker, I tap into the universal life force energy and allow it to flow through me, facilitating healing for others. This channeling process is not just about directing energy; it's about being open and receptive to the frequencies that surround us. I've realized that every individual has the potential to be a channel; it's about recognizing and harnessing this ability within myself. This recognition empowers me to see myself as capable of facilitating healing for those around me, reminding me that my presence can be a source of comfort and transformation. I often visualize myself as a vessel, letting the energy flow freely, transforming my intentions into healing light that impacts others positively.

I've learned that the flow of energy is fundamental to healing. It's a dynamic process that involves not just moving energy but also understanding its rhythms and patterns. It's something I call the Cosmic Dance. I've practiced moving and directing energy intentionally, whether through my hands or focused thought. Grounding myself has become crucial; when I connect to the Earth, I feel more stable and balanced. I often visualize energy flowing through my body like a river, cleansing and revitalizing me. I even imagine the cascading cleansing sounds of a waterfall or running rivers, preparing me to share this energy with others. I've also discovered that energy can be influenced by my emotions and thoughts, so I strive to maintain a positive mindset and clear intention before engaging in any healing work. This is why frequency plays such a crucial role. After all, everything is energy, and energy is always moving; movement happens in terms of frequency. This awareness has deepened my understanding of how interconnected we all are through energy, and I feel honored to be a conduit for that flow.

Setting intentions has become a vital part of my practice. I've learned that aligning my intentions with a specific purpose enhances the healing process. Before I begin a healing session, I take a moment to center myself, focusing on what I wish to accomplish. I often write down my intentions in a journal, crafting affirmations that resonate with my heart and soul. Creating a sacred space—whether through lighting candles, playing soft music, or arranging crystals—helps me attract focused energy. I've found that when I set clear intentions, the healing energy flows more freely and powerfully, guiding both me and the recipients of my energy toward the desired outcome. This intentionality gives my healing a sense of purpose, making it not just a practice but a profound connection with those I seek to help.

Connecting with higher realms has been transformative for me. I often reach out to spirit guides, angels, or higher consciousness to enhance my healing abilities. This connection brings additional wisdom and support that deepens my practice. During meditation, I visualize a bright light above me, representing the higher realms. I call upon my guides, asking for their assistance and guidance in my healing work. Their presence feels comforting, reminding me that I am never alone on this journey. This connection has taught me to trust my intuition more deeply. I've learned to listen to the whispers of my inner voice, which often guides me to what is needed in each moment. By tuning into this higher guidance, I can offer more profound healing experiences to those I work with.

Empathy has taught me to understand and resonate with the emotions of others, creating a safe space for healing. It's a powerful gift that allows me to feel what others are experiencing, enabling me to connect with them on a deeper level. When I sit with someone who is struggling, I open my heart and invite their emotions into my awareness, allowing myself to truly be present with them. This ability to empathize amplifies my compassion, which is essential for facilitating healing. I strive to develop these qualities further, recognizing how they help heal emotional wounds and foster deeper relationships in my life. I often remind myself that being a lightworker is not just about channeling energy; it's about being a loving presence, offering comfort and understanding to those in need.

I've realized that prioritizing self-care is essential for maintaining my energy levels and emotional balance as a lightworker. Without self-care, I risk burnout and diminished effectiveness in my healing work. I engage in regular meditation, finding solace in the stillness and clarity it brings. Spending time in nature is another crucial aspect of my self-care routine; I feel rejuvenated by the sights, sounds, and energies of the natural world. Engaging in activities that bring me joy—like painting, dancing, or simply reading—helps me recharge. Additionally, I practice energy clearing techniques, like smudging with sage or using crystals to cleanse my aura, ensuring that my energy field remains clear and vibrant. Another go-to is lighting incense. I've learned that when I take care of myself, I am better equipped to help others, making self-care an integral part of my light working journey.

Exploring various healing modalities has enriched my journey as a lightworker. Each modality offers unique techniques and benefits, whether it's Reiki, sound healing, or crystal therapy. I've discovered that I resonate with certain modalities more than others, allowing me to channel energy in ways that feel authentic to me. For example, I find that working with crystals amplifies my healing energy, and I often incorporate them into my sessions. I appreciate how sound healing, with its vibrational frequencies, can shift energy and create a harmonious atmosphere. I've learned to appreciate the different ways I can channel energy and encourage others to explore modalities that resonate with them. This exploration opens doors to new experiences and insights, enhancing my effectiveness as a lightworker.

I've experienced firsthand how channeling positivity and healing creates a ripple effect. One act of kindness or healing can impact not just individuals but entire communities, fostering collective healing and upliftment. I often reflect on the stories of those who have been positively influenced by a simple gesture or moment of compassion. This realization motivates me to be mindful of my actions and words, knowing that they can inspire others in ways I may not even see. Sharing these stories reminds me of our interconnectedness and inspires me to play a role in uplifting society. I understand that every positive thought, word, or action contributes to a greater collective energy, and I strive to be a beacon of that light in the world.

In my journey, I've come to understand the importance of acknowledging and integrating my shadow aspects to achieve wholeness. Embracing my darkness allows me to experience deeper healing and understanding. I've realized that my challenges and struggles are not something to be ashamed of but rather essential parts of my growth. I encourage myself to confront my fears and limiting beliefs, knowing that this process enhances my ability to empathize with the struggles of others. By embracing my shadow, I become more authentic and relatable, allowing me to connect more deeply with those I aim to help. This balance of light and shadow enriches my journey as a lightworker, reminding me that we are all multifaceted beings on a path of evolution.

Every step of my journey as a lightworker has been unique, filled with challenges and revelations. I find sharing personal anecdotes and insights can inspire others. I reflect on the challenges I've faced, such as moments of self-doubt or feeling overwhelmed, and how I've grown from them. The breakthroughs I've experienced—those moments of clarity or connection—have shaped who I am today. I share these stories to show that the path of a lightworker is not always easy, but it is profoundly rewarding. I encourage others to embrace their own journeys, knowing that every experience contributes to their growth and purpose.

Visual imagery enhances my connection to the concepts I'm exploring. I often evoke vivid imagery in my mind, such as light surrounding a person or healing energy resembling gentle waves washing over someone in distress. I use this imagery not only for my practice but also to communicate these concepts to others. By inviting others to imagine these experiences, I create a shared understanding of the beauty of channeling healing energy. For instance, I guide them to visualize a warm, golden light enveloping them, filling them with peace and comfort. This practice fosters a sense of connection and encourages them to engage with their healing journey.

Practical exercises have become a vital part of my practice. I enjoy engaging in guided meditations and visualizations that help me connect with my healing abilities. For example, I might lead myself through a meditation where I envision a healing light surrounding me and extending to others, feeling the energy flow through me like a gentle current. These exercises not only deepen my connection to my inner healer but also provide me with tools to share with others. I encourage regular practice, knowing that the more we engage with these techniques, the more we strengthen our ability to channel healing energy and support those around us.

Serving others while maintaining your own energy

As a lightworker, I've come to understand that setting boundaries is essential for maintaining my energy and well-being. Initially, I thought being compassionate meant always being available to others. However, I learned that without clear boundaries, I risk becoming drained and resentful. Establishing boundaries involves recognizing my limits—emotionally, physically, and energetically and communicating them clearly to others. For instance, I now allow myself time after healing sessions to recharge, letting others know that I may not respond immediately. Setting these boundaries creates a sacred space where I can serve others without depleting myself.

Grounding techniques are crucial for me as a lightworker. They help me stay centered and balanced amidst the various energies I encounter. One effective method I practice is spending time in nature—as often as possible—visualizing roots extending from my feet into the Earth to anchor me. Mindful breathing is another grounding technique I use, where I focus on my breath and visualize it washing over me, releasing any negative energy. I also incorporate grounding crystals, like black tourmaline or shungite, into my daily routine to enhance my connection with the Earth. These practices help me maintain clarity and stability, ensuring I can serve from a grounded place.

Regularly clearing my energy is vital for my well-being as a lightworker. I've learned that I can absorb negative energies during interactions, which can lead to feeling overwhelmed, even if I'm not actively assisting someone. To counteract this, I incorporate rituals like smudging with sage to cleanse my space and my aura. I also use visualization techniques, imagining a bright light surrounding me to absorb any negative energy. Taking a long shower is another practice I enjoy, as the water purifies my energy. By integrating these energy-clearing methods into my life, I create a clean vibrational space that supports my work.

Mindfulness practices have transformed my approach as a lightworker. By cultivating present awareness, I become attuned to my emotional and energetic states. I dedicate time to meditation, allowing my thoughts to flow without judgment, which helps me process my experiences. I also practice mindful listening in conversations, focusing on truly hearing others without formulating my response.

Additionally, I engage in mindful movement through yoga or tai chi, connecting with my body and releasing tension. These practices help me stay grounded and aware, enabling me to serve from a place of authenticity.

Prioritizing self-care rituals is essential for my sustainability as a lightworker. I've learned that I must nurture myself to pour into others effectively. I schedule regular self-care days where I engage in activities that nourish my soul, like spending time in nature or pursuing creative interests. Daily practices, such as journaling and reflection, allow me to process my emotions and reinforce my commitment to self-care. I also create small rituals to honor my journey, like lighting a candle and setting intentions. By embracing self-care as a priority, I build a strong foundation for my work as a lightworker.

Finding balance between giving and receiving has been a significant lesson for me. I've realized that while it's important to serve others, I must also allow myself to receive support. I practice gratitude daily, acknowledging the blessings in my life. I seek connections with others, whether through support groups or friendships, and I've learned that leaning on others is okay. To reinforce this balance, I engage in activities that bring me joy and fulfillment, nurturing my own passions. By embracing the flow of energy in my life, I create equilibrium that sustains my work.

Cultivating gratitude has transformed my perspective as a lightworker. I focus on the abundance in my life, which creates a positive energy that fuels my journey. I keep a gratitude journal, writing down three things I appreciate each day, as I've previously mentioned. This simple practice shifts my focus from scarcity to abundance, reminding me of the beauty in my life. Gratitude helps me maintain a positive mindset, enabling me to serve others from a place of joy and fulfillment.

Active listening is a skill I've developed to enhance my interactions as a lightworker. When engaging with others, I strive to be fully present, giving them my undivided attention. I focus on understanding their feelings and experiences without judgment. This practice creates a safe space for healing, allowing the other person to feel heard and validated. By employing active listening, I foster deeper connections and enhance the quality of my service. Shaman Om used to say, "Healing begins when you feel heard."

Emotional awareness is a crucial aspect of my journey as a lightworker. I've learned to recognize and honor my emotions, understanding that they provide valuable insights into my state of being. By tuning into my feelings, I can better understand when I need to recharge or when to set boundaries. I also encourage others to explore their emotional landscapes, helping them identify and process their feelings. This practice promotes healing and growth, both for myself and those I serve.

As a lightworker, I embrace the importance of continuous learning. I seek out workshops, books, and resources that expand my knowledge and deepen my understanding of healing practices. I also engage in discussions with fellow lightworkers, exchanging ideas and techniques. This commitment to growth not only enhances my skills but also enriches my ability to serve others. By staying open to new perspectives, I ensure that my journey remains dynamic and fulfilling.

Deepening my spiritual connection has been transformative in my work as a lightworker. I explore various spiritual practices, such as meditation, prayer, and rituals, to cultivate a stronger connection to the divine. By fostering this relationship, I invite guidance and support into my life, enhancing my ability to serve others. I also encourage those I work with to explore their spiritual paths, helping them connect with their own inner wisdom. This shared journey fosters a sense of community and collective healing.

Chapter 7 The Balance of Day and Night

The Duality of Existence: Light and Shadow Within

I am both the light that guides and the shadow that follows. People think of darkness as something to be feared, something empty and hollow. They believe that to stand in the light is to be safe. But I know better. Darkness is not an absence; it is a presence, vast and knowing, filled with truths too raw for the untrained soul to bear. It does not coddle. It does not lie. It strips away the illusions people build to make themselves comfortable, exposing what is real, no matter how painful. And yet, the light—the light is warmth, a promise, a purpose. It is the part of me that longs to heal, to guide, to awaken those still trapped in the dream of this world. When I stand in the light, I feel the pull of creation, of something greater than myself calling me forward. It sings in a way the darkness never does, filling me with a clarity that makes me feel whole.

But light, for all its beauty, can be just as blinding as the deepest abyss. In its demand for purity, it leaves no room for the jagged edges of existence. It can burn just as easily as it illuminates. I have walked too far in both directions. There

81

were times when I let the shadows wrap around me like a cloak, their power intoxicating, their whispers promising freedom. I reveled in the weightlessness of it, the way the darkness strips away all need for pretense. But it does not love. It does not comfort. It only reveals. And so, I have also fled into the light, trying to purge myself of the things I could not bear to face, hoping its radiance would cleanse me. But neither side holds the answer alone. I am not meant to be one or the other. I exist in the space where they meet. I am the bridge between them. The balance. The storm before the calm, the dusk before the dawn. I am betwixt. What am I, if not the proof that both can exist within the same soul?

The Physical vs. Spiritual Self

I exist in this body, in this world. I feel the pull of gravity, the ache of hunger, the exhaustion that settles into my bones. I breathe, I bleed, I wake and sleep like anyone else. And yet, this body feels like an illusion, like something borrowed, something I wear rather than something I am. The "meat-suit." There are moments when the veil between worlds grows thin, when I feel the weight of my spirit stretching beyond the boundaries of flesh. My consciousness expands, slipping into a vastness that exists outside of time, outside of form, like a trance, except while being present in the moment without the need for meditation to achieve the trance-like frequency. In those moments, I am more than human. I am something ancient, something infinite, not bound by time or place. I remember things that were never spoken, truths that were never taught. The knowing simply is.

But then I return. I blink, and the vastness shrinks back into the confines of a body too small to contain it. The weight of this existence presses down again. Hunger, fatigue, the slow drag of time. I do not resent it, but I do not belong to it either. I am caught between two states of being, never fully one or the other, always looking for a way to maintain balance. It is an exile, in a way—to be awake in a world that is still asleep, to know that I am more than this and yet be bound to the limits of flesh, to feel the pull of something greater and still be forced to exist in the mundane, while forced to travel into the boundless edges of time without a warning for its demand. I wonder, sometimes, if there will come a day when I no longer need this form, when I can step beyond it entirely. But until then, I walk this strange in-between, caught between what I am and what I seem to be, witnessing the evolution of consciousness in the divine balance of all that is, all that has been, and all it could be.

The Seen and the Unseen

People walk through this world blind, unaware of the

currents that move beneath them. They believe in what they can touch, what they can measure. They chase certainty, comfort, permanence, all the while oblivious to the shifting, impermanent nature of everything around them, the invisible forces that shift in frequencies not captured by the average naked eye. I see differently. I see the strings that weave through existence, the patterns hidden beneath the surface of reality. I see the lies people tell themselves, the fears they try to ignore. I see the echoes of things that have not yet come to pass, the imprints of what has already been, not bound by physics while thriving in the quantum realm.

But how do I explain this sight to those who do not wish to see? I have tried before. I have spoken in careful words, tried to show them the edges of the truth without tearing away the veil too quickly. Some listen, their minds opening just enough to glimpse what lies beyond their understanding. But most look at me with confusion—or worse, with fear. Some call me wise for the insight. Some call me strange. Some call me lost. And the rest call me crazy. They do not realize that I am none of these things. I am simply awake, experiencing life without veils, caressing multiple states of mind at once.

I have learned to walk quietly, to offer glimpses, not revelations, to plant seeds rather than force open closed doors. I cannot make someone see if they are not ready. But I watch. I wait. And when I see that spark in another, when I see the recognition in their eyes, the first flicker of awakening, I know my path is not in vain. That is enough for me.

Love and Solitude

I have tried to love. I have tried to let people in, to make space for them in the vastness of my existence. But love, for someone like me, is not simple. It is not a meeting of two people. It is the collision of entire worlds, entire ways of seeing and understanding. And my world is not easy to step into. To love is to be seen. And that is where the problem begins.

Most people love what they understand, what fits into the framework of their reality. They want love to be familiar, to be something they can grasp. But I do not fit into neat definitions, into easy explanations. I do not experience love in the way most do. I do not love lightly, and I do not know how to be half-seen. Yet, I continue to try.

I see beyond the surface. I sense the fractures in people, the wounds they don't acknowledge, what stage they are in on their karmic cycle, unhealed traumas, the shadows they carry. I know when they are speaking truths and when they are dressing their words in masks. For instance, I see the wound in one dimension oscillating around their mask, which dances in a different frequency. And the more I see, the harder it is to pretend. I learn to embrace them through both pain and light, accepting the duality, longing for someone to reciprocate.

I have tried to silence this part of myself, to love as others do—to accept, to overlook, to exist in the illusion of simplicity. But love is never simple when you know too much. I feel shifts in energy before words are spoken, long before the other part develops awareness in their own shift. I sense hesitation before it turns into distance. I know when a heart is already pulling away, even when the body remains close. And how do I explain that I can feel it happening? How do I tell someone that I am watching them drift from me in real-time, that I know before they do that they are leaving?

People think love is about connection, about finding someone who makes you feel whole. But I have never been incomplete. I have never needed another person to complete me—only to meet me, to stand beside me without fear as I delve deeper into the unseen currents. But who stands beside someone like me? I have loved people who have loved me in return, but there is always a point where they hesitate. A moment where they look at me and realize I am not something they can hold in place, that I am vast and shifting, that I am too much and yet not enough in the ways they expect.

And so, I have walked away before they could. Not because I wanted to. Not because I did not love them. But because I saw the moment coming when they would choose to leave, and I could not bear to watch it unfold in slow motion. So I walk alone. Not because I wish to, but because solitude is the only place where I do not have to make myself smaller. Here, in the quiet, I do not have to filter my existence through the expectations of others. I do not have to soften my edges or pretend I do not feel the things I feel.

But there are moments—moments when the weight of solitude becomes unbearable, when I long for someone who understands, someone who does not need explanations, who does not fear the depth of what I am. Is it possible? To find a love that does not ask me to be less? To find someone who sees me, truly sees me, and does not flinch? I do not know. But if such a soul exists, I will find them. Or perhaps, they will find me. And maybe then, I will no longer have to walk alone.

Exploring Ancient Philosophies on Balance

Balance has always been a central theme in spiritual and philosophical traditions, often misunderstood as a static state of being. Through my explorations and meditative practices, I have come to see that balance is dynamic, requiring movement, awareness, and adaptability. My journey into this understanding began with profound visions of two ancient philosophies: Yin and Yang and Ma'at.

Yin and Yang: The Flow of Duality

My first encounter with the philosophy of Yin and Yang came during a deep meditation, where I sought to elevate my consciousness. In this altered state, I was blessed to witness the interconnectedness of all life—an intricate web that spans throughout history. I saw that every existence has had to maintain a constant balance, a rhythm of opposites that define the universe. This revelation opened my eyes to the dynamic flow of energy that characterizes existence. Yin embodies the passive, dark, and receptive forces, while Yang represents the active, bright, and assertive aspects. Initially, I viewed these as separate forces, but my vision revealed their interdependence.

I recognized that imbalance arises not from the presence of one force but from the resistance to the natural ebb and flow between them. As I reflected on this during my daily life, I began to appreciate the necessity of honoring both energies. Society often overvalues Yang—productivity, action, and control—while neglecting the importance of Yin—rest, intuition, and surrender. I realized I had also fallen into this trap, pushing myself relentlessly while disregarding my need for stillness. It was only when I embraced the restorative aspects of Yin that I could move forward with clarity and purpose.

Ma'at: The Cosmic Scale of Truth

Months later, during another meditation, I encountered Ma'at, the Egyptian concept of balance and cosmic order. In this vision, she introduced herself to me, embodying truth, justice, and harmony. Ma'at represents a state of alignment with natural laws and ethical responsibility. In my vision, Ma'at taught me about the significance of the feather—the symbol of truth and lightness of being. She guided me through the process of balancing a single feather against a person's heart to reveal their true essence. This imagery has stayed with me, prompting introspection about my actions and choices.

The weighing of the heart ceremony, where one's heart is assessed against the feather of Ma'at in the afterlife, resonates deeply with me. It emphasizes that inner balance is crucial for personal and spiritual evolution. The notion that our hearts must remain light with integrity and honesty motivates me to reflect on my interactions with others and the world. I have come to see that maintaining balance extends beyond individual pursuits. Ma'at serves as a reminder that our actions contribute to a larger cosmic order. As I strive for personal harmony, I must also consider how my choices affect those around me and the planet. Everything connects.

Applying These Principles Today

Through my encounters with Yin and Yang and Ma'at, I have gained valuable insights into the nature of balance. I have learned that it is not a destination but a continuous journey requiring constant adjustment and awareness. From Yin and Yang, I have come to understand that balance permeates every aspect of life. It is not simply a matter of opposing forces; it reflects the intricate interplay of highs and lows, joy and sorrow, work and rest. Just as winter needs summer to create the cycle of seasons, we need challenges to appreciate our triumphs.

Each test we face requires breaks to restore our energy, allowing us to emerge stronger and more resilient. This principle extends beyond mere duality; it embodies the understanding that everything in existence seeks equilibrium. Flowers need both sun and rain to bloom fully, just as our lives require moments of light and shadow to foster growth. Recognizing this cyclical nature has taught me to embrace the full spectrum of my experiences, understanding that each moment contributes to the larger tapestry of my journey, embodying a deep-rooted sense of gratitude, a key component in the dynamic of who I must remain, while I strive to restore balance in my daily life.

From Ma'at, I remind myself to align my thoughts and actions with my deepest truths. The practice of weighing the heart against the feather has encouraged me to live with integrity and lightness, ensuring that my choices reflect the harmony I seek. Balance is not about achieving perfection; it is an ongoing practice, a rhythm, a dance between forces that shape our existence. My visions of Yin and Yang and Ma'at have profoundly influenced my spiritual journey, reminding me that their wisdom is as relevant today as it was in ancient times.

The Day Walker's Role as a Bridge Between Opposites

Reflecting on my journey as a Day Walker, I realize that it embodies a continuous quest for balance, akin to the interplay of light and shadow. Each day offers an opportunity to engage with the wisdom of ancient teachings, particularly those of Ma'at, whose principles guide me toward truth and harmony. Ma'at represents order, balance, and justice, serving as a compass for my actions and decisions. In moments of chaos, I find solace in her teachings, reminding me that even in turmoil, there exists a possibility for restoration.

This quest for balance is mirrored in the ancient symbol of Yin Yang, illustrating how darkness and light are not adversaries but partners in the intricate dance of existence.

Each complements the other, creating a richness that is deeper than either can achieve alone. And so, I bridge them together. Throughout my life, I have encountered moments where I felt caught between opposing forces—times when joy felt distant, overshadowed by fear or uncertainty. Navigating these challenges, I learned that struggles often serve as bridges to greater understanding.

Rather than resisting the darkness, I began to embrace it, allowing it to reveal hidden lessons. In those moments of feeling lost, I discovered the strength to seek my truth, ultimately guiding me toward clarity. In addition to Ma'at, I find profound guidance in the principles of the Eightfold Path and the Four Noble Truths. The Eightfold Path encourages me to cultivate right understanding and right action, providing a framework that aligns my aspirations with my daily actions. The Four Noble Truths illuminate the nature of suffering and the path to liberation, reminding me that acknowledging suffering is a vital step toward healing.

These teachings foster compassion for myself and others, deepening my connection to the human experience. The concept of Dharma also resonates within me, guiding me to honor my unique path and purpose. Understanding my Dharma encourages me to embrace the duality of existence, recognizing that my journey intertwines with those around me. Each of us plays a role in the greater tapestry of life, and in honoring our Dharma, we contribute to a more harmonious world.

As I navigate my role as a Day Walker, I often turn to mindfulness practices to find clarity. These moments of stillness allow me to connect with the present and reflect on what balance means in various aspects of my life. Through these practices, I have found greater understanding and growth, which informs my interactions with others. Working with Thoth, the ancient deity of wisdom, has enriched my spiritual journey. His guidance reinforces the idea that knowledge is a powerful tool for bridging opposites.

In exploring ancient teachings, I continually seek wisdom that resonates with my experiences and inspires balance in my life. Finally, as I consider the symbols surrounding us, I reflect on the ancient Egyptian art that depicts the interplay of light and dark. Each symbol holds a story and a lesson, inviting contemplation. These images serve as reminders of our journey as Day Walkers, each representing the delicate balance we strive to achieve.

I reflect on my role as a bridge within my community. Embracing the spirit of a Day Walker allows me to foster connection and understanding in a world often fragmented. By celebrating both the light and dark that shape us, we can navigate our paths with greater clarity and purpose, my deepest wish.

Chapter 8 Living as a Day Walker

Bridging Two Worlds

In our busy lives, finding balance often feels like a juggling act. We manage daily responsibilities, relationships, and dreams while craving a deeper connection to who we really are. As Day Walkers, we navigate the delicate dance between our spiritual selves and the material world, understanding that these aspects are deeply connected. Daily practices can create harmony between these two sides of life. From the moment we wake up to when we wind down at night, simple actions can link our earthly experiences with the spiritual guidance around us. Here are some things I have found helpful with the guidance of my personal shaman, Shaman Om, and the support of my deepest friend, Shai. Through mindful eating, tapping into creativity, and spending time in nature, these practices invite us to feel more whole. They turn everyday moments into opportunities for growth, reminding us that our spiritual journey is intertwined with the life we live. Embracing these practices enhances our existence as Day Walkers, blending the spiritual and material in a way that feels authentic and enriching.

Meditation: Grounding in Intention

Every morning, I carve out a few sacred moments to sit in stillness, allowing the world to quiet around me. As I close my eyes and take deep, intentional breaths, I feel the weight of the night lift. This practice helps me connect with my innermost self and set intentions for the day ahead. I visualize a golden light surrounding me, symbolizing both spiritual guidance and the grounding energy of the earth. This moment of mindfulness is a gentle reminder that I can embrace both the spiritual and material aspects of my life with grace.

Cultivating a Positive Mindset

After meditation, I reach for my gratitude journal. With pen in hand, I jot down three things I'm thankful for, whether it's the warmth of the sun streaming through my window, the laughter of my children, or the simple pleasure of a good cup of coffee. This practice shifts my perspective, setting the tone for the day, inviting positive energy. I remind myself that acknowledging the abundance in my life helps me harmonize my spiritual beliefs with my material experiences. Each entry serves as a touchstone, grounding me in appreciation and drawing me closer to the life I wish to cultivate.

Conscious Consumption: Connecting with My Food

As I prepare my breakfast, I make a conscious effort to be present with my food. I appreciate the vibrant colors of the fruits and vegetables, the textures of the grains, and the nourishment they provide. I often pause to reflect on the journey of my food from the earth to my plate and consider the impact it has on my body and spirit. This practice of mindful eating deepens my connection to the material world while honoring the sacredness of nourishment. I find that when I eat with intention, I feel more energized and aligned.

Rituals Before Meals: Honoring the Moment

Before each meal, I create a small ritual to honor the nourishment I'm about to receive. It could be as simple as lighting a candle or saying a few words of gratitude for the food and those who contributed to it. This moment transforms an ordinary meal into a sacred experience, allowing me to integrate spiritual mindfulness into my daily routine. By acknowledging the significance of my food, I create a bridge between my spiritual values and the physical act of eating.

Outdoor Time: Embracing the Elements

Each day, I prioritize spending time outdoors; usually, it's a brisk walk in the park. I breathe in the fresh air, feeling the sun on my skin and the ground beneath my feet. This connection to nature nourishes my spirit and reminds me of my place in the world. I find that immersing myself in the beauty of nature helps me harmonize the spiritual and material aspects of my life, reminding me of the cycles of life and the interconnectedness of all things. I focus on what I see and hear while bathing in its energy.

Nature Meditation: Finding Peace in the Wild

When I'm in nature, I sometimes practice a form of meditation, allowing the sounds of birds and rustling leaves to envelop me. I focus on my breath and let my thoughts flow like water, becoming one with the environment around me. This practice of connecting with nature not only brings me peace but also strengthens my spiritual awareness. I recognize that the earth holds wisdom and energy that can guide me on my journey, and I strive to honor that connection in my daily life.

Art and Creativity: Channels for the Soul

I find immense joy in engaging with creative practices that allow me to express my spiritual insights. Whether it's painting, writing, playing music, or simply coloring, I view creativity as a sacred act. When I create, I tap into a flow of energy that transcends the ordinary, connecting me to something greater. These moments of artistic expression become a dance between my inner world and the outer reality, helping me to bridge the gap between spirituality and material existence.

Breathwork: Harnessing the Power of Breath

Throughout my day, I incorporate breathwork, especially during moments of stress or overwhelm. Taking a few deep, intentional breaths allows me to center myself and reconnect with my inner wisdom. I visualize my breath as a bridge, linking my physical body with my spiritual essence. This practice reminds me that I have the power to ground myself in any situation, harmonizing my emotional state with the present moment.

Body Awareness: Listening to My Inner Self

Practicing body awareness has been transformative for me. I take a moment each day to check in with how I'm feeling physically and spiritually. This might involve a gentle body scan, where I consciously relax each part of my body and release any tension. By tuning into my physical sensations, I cultivate a deeper understanding of how my emotions and thoughts impact my body. This connection helps me find balance and encourages a holistic approach to my well-being.

End-of-Day Review: Celebrating My Journey

As the day winds down, I set aside time for reflection. I sit quietly, reviewing the experiences of the day—what went well, what challenged me, and how I felt spiritually and materially. This practice allows me to celebrate my successes and learn from my challenges. By acknowledging my growth, I reinforce the connection between my spiritual practices and daily life, fostering a sense of harmony as I move forward.

Dream Journaling: Tapping into the Subconscious

I keep a journal by my bedside to record my dreams, knowing they often hold insights and messages from my subconscious. Each morning, I take a few moments to write down what I remember, reflecting on how these dreams relate to my waking life. This practice helps me integrate spiritual lessons into my daily experiences, reminding me that the boundaries between the spiritual and material are often blurred. By honoring my dreams, I nurture a deeper understanding of myself.

Community Engagement: Strengthening Connections

Engaging in acts of kindness within my community is a vital part of my daily practice. Whether offering a listening ear to a friend or simply smiling at a stranger, I find that these small gestures create ripples of positivity. By giving back, I connect with the spirit of generosity and compassion, harmonizing my spiritual values with my material life. Each act of service reminds me that we are all interconnected, and that my contributions matter.

Personal Altar: A Reflection of My Values

Creating a personal altar, a sacred space, is a cherished practice for me. I gather objects that resonate with my spiritual beliefs and material aspirations—crystals, photos, meaningful symbols, and mementos. Each item holds significance, serving as a visual representation of my journey. I often spend time at my altar, reflecting on my intentions and expressing gratitude for the abundance in my life. This sacred space reminds me of the harmony I strive to cultivate between my spiritual and material worlds.

Daily Affirmations: Empowering My Path

Affirmations have been a cornerstone of my journey, providing a powerful tool for transformation. They taught me how to express my worth and potential rather than succumbing to negative self-talk and doubt that often linger in the lower frequencies of thought.

By consciously choosing affirmations, I learned to reshape my inner dialogue, replacing critical voices with words of encouragement and love. This practice not only helps me stay aligned with my intentions but also plays a significant role in balancing my chakras. Each affirmation resonates with specific energy centers within my body, helping to release blockages and restore flow.

For instance, affirmations centered on self-love and acceptance open my heart chakra, allowing me to connect more deeply with my emotions and those around me. Similarly, affirmations focused on creativity and expression empower my throat chakra, enabling me to communicate my truth authentically.

Incorporating affirmations into my daily routine has become a ritual. I often recite them in the morning to set a positive tone for the day or during meditation to deepen my connection with my inner self. The act of voicing these affirmations reinforces my beliefs and intentions, reminding me that I am capable of manifesting my desires and navigating life's challenges with grace and confidence. It's become my second nature.

Additionally, the practices discussed in earlier sections contribute to my overall chakral energy balance. Mindful eating nourishes my body, creative expression fuels my sacral chakra, and time spent in nature grounds me, promoting a sense of stability. Together, these practices and affirmations create a holistic approach to well-being, aligning my physical, emotional, and spiritual selves.

As I continue to embrace daily affirmations, I feel empowered to walk my path with intention, resilience, and joy. Each affirmation becomes a beacon of light, guiding me through the complexities of life and reminding me of the strength that resides within.

How I Navigate Challenges While Staying True to My Path; A Quiet Strength: Holding Light Without Losing Myself; For a long time, I thought that being a source of light meant giving everything I had—pouring myself into others, stretching beyond my limits, and offering my energy freely, no matter how depleted I became, even if nothing was left. I didn't notice how often I was running on fumes, pushing forward even when I was empty. It wasn't just exhaustion; it was a deep spiritual depletion, a hollowness that made me question if I could keep going. My deepest friend and shaman pointed out that I was too comfortable running on fumes. Although I heard this often, it didn't quite click right away, not without struggle. I learned the hard way: light cannot sustain itself without fuel.

I had to confront the truth: being a light does not mean burning myself out. It does not mean sacrificing my well-being for the sake of others. I had to find a way to pour without being left empty. That's when I truly embraced spiritual hygiene—not just as a practice, but as a necessity. Grounding myself, tending to my own healing, and creating rituals of renewal became my way of restoring balance. I had to learn that self-care wasn't selfish; it was survival. By taking the time to replenish, I could give without breaking. I could shine without dimming.

This journey is ongoing. Some days, I still find myself slipping into old patterns, giving too much before remembering to refill. But I see the difference now. I recognize when I need to pause, breathe, and restore my energy. It's no longer about just holding the light; it's about sustaining it. In doing so, I've discovered that my light isn't something that can be taken from me. It's something I can nurture. And when I care for it, it shines even brighter, not just for others, but for myself.

Between Sun and Shadow: Walking with Grace

For a time, I embraced the philosophy of "positive vibes only," believing that if I surrounded myself with light and positivity, I could ward off darkness and negativity. I filled my life with affirmations, joyful moments, and uplifting thoughts. It felt empowering at first, and I thought I was cultivating a beautiful existence. But as I pushed away the shadows, I realized that my journey was not as simple as I had hoped. Ignoring the shadows didn't make them disappear; that was a temporary illusion that only embraced half of my identity. The darkness lingered just beneath the surface, whispering truths I wasn't ready to face, my shadow.

In my quest for relentless positivity, I lost touch with the parts of myself that needed healing. I almost lost myself in the process, drowning in an unrealistic expectation of constant happiness. I felt fragmented, struggling to reconcile the darkness I feared with the light I so desperately wanted to embody. It was then that I understood the necessity of addressing the shadows. I had to confront the pain, the fears, and the uncertainties I had pushed away. It was a difficult journey, as I ventured into depths I had long avoided. The shadows were uncomfortable, often chaotic, but they held essential truths about my identity, my past, and my resilience.

I learned that to grow, I had to embrace them instead of fighting against them. This exploration led me back to the concept of yin and yang again—the idea that light and dark coexist in harmony. I realized that I didn't have to choose between being positive or acknowledging my struggles; I could embody both, and so I did. Now, I walk with grace between these two worlds, most days, understanding that neither defines me completely. The light nourishes my spirit, while the shadows provide the depth and richness of my experience.

I have learned to honor both, allowing myself to feel joy and pain, hope and fear, love and loss. By integrating these aspects, I find balance in my journey. I can be radiant without dismissing the lessons from the shadows. Each step I take, whether in light or darkness, is a part of my unfolding path. I embrace the complexity of my existence, knowing that walking with grace means accepting all of who I am, both the sun and the shadow.

The Soft Echo of Truth: Staying Rooted in Who I Am

The world is full of voices—loud, insistent, demanding. They tell me who I should be, how I should live, what I should believe. It is easy to get lost in them, to feel like my own voice is too soft to matter. But beneath all that noise, there is something steady, something unshaken. My truth. It does not shout. It does not beg for attention. It waits. It waits for me to be still enough to hear it, to trust it, to follow it.

I have spent years doubting myself, bending to fit expectations, questioning my intuition, despite the reliability it shares with me. But every time I return to stillness, I remember. I remember that I do not have to explain myself to be valid. I do not have to prove my worth. I do not have to convince anyone of my path. This shift allowed me to step into my role with more clarity, confidence, and a new depth. I root myself in my truth, knowing that it will guide me, even when others don't understand, even when the world tries to pull me in different directions. My truth is mine, and that is enough.

Gentle Footsteps on a Winding Path

As I tread along the winding path of my journey, I've come to embrace the idea that healing is not a straight line but rather a beautiful spiral. I vividly recall a picture I once encountered— a simple yet profound image of a spiral, elegantly illustrating the cyclical nature of our experiences. This imagery resonated deeply with me, reflecting the essence of how we encounter the same themes in life, but each time, we do so with deeper clarity and understanding. Life, like a spiral, invites us to revisit aspects of ourselves that may feel familiar, yet each return brings new insights.

I learned that these repetitions are not failures or signs of stagnation; instead, they are opportunities for growth, allowing us to delve deeper into our healing process. With each turn of the spiral, I discovered layers of wisdom previously obscured, enabling me to see my experiences from a fresh perspective. As I embraced this concept, I began to navigate my path with gentler footsteps. I learned to honor the twists and turns, understanding that the winding nature of my journey is what enriches my experience.

Instead of rushing to the next destination, I became more attuned to the moments along the way. I cultivated patience and compassion for myself, recognizing that healing unfolds in its own time and rhythm, inherently. With each gentle step,

I engaged with the emotions and memories that arose, allowing them to surface without judgment. Remaining neutral, I learned to sit with discomfort, understanding that it was often in these moments of vulnerability that the most profound healing could occur. The spiral taught me that I could confront old wounds with a newfound perspective, transforming them into sources of strength rather than reminders of pain. I learned to trust the gentle footsteps on my winding path. I embraced the spiral as a guide, offering me the clarity and depth needed to navigate the complexities of healing. Each turn brought me closer to my authentic self, illuminating the way forward with love and compassion.

The Power of Reflection: Grounding in Self-Awareness

In the dance of light and shadow, self-awareness emerges as a vital tool for navigating the complexities of being a Day Walker. It's the compass that guides me through the chaotic landscapes of emotions and experiences, helping me discern when to lean into the light and when to honor the shadows. Yet, achieving this self-awareness is a journey in itself, one that requires patience, honesty, and a willingness to look inward. Reflection has become a sacred practice for me. I take the time to pause, to sit with my thoughts and emotions, and to understand what they are trying to tell me. This process often involves journaling, meditating, or simply being present in nature, allowing the rhythm of the earth to ground me. During these moments, I tune in to the whispers of my heart and mind, giving space for truths to emerge.

Through this practice, I've discovered that self-awareness isn't just about identifying my feelings. It's about understanding their roots. Why do I feel this way? What experiences or beliefs shape my reactions? Is it a helpful coping mechanism? Each reflection brings me closer to my authentic self, allowing me to peel back the layers of conditioning and societal expectations that often cloud my perception. Grounding is essential in this process, a lesson Shaman Om often reminds me of.

It's easy to get swept away in the tides of external influences, societal pressures, and expectations. With his guidance, I've learned to create a foundation of stability within myself. Practices like breathwork, meditation, and connecting with nature remind me of my true essence. These moments of grounding anchor me, allowing me to navigate life's storms with clarity and resilience.

As I cultivate self-awareness, I also embrace my authenticity. I no longer feel the need to conform to ideals of perfection or suppress the parts of myself that don't fit neatly into a box. I've come to appreciate the beautiful messiness of being human—the joys, the struggles, the triumphs, and the failures. Each facet contributes to the tapestry of my multifaceted existence. This journey of self-discovery has taught me that being a Day Walker means embracing my full spectrum. I honor my light and shadows, my strength and vulnerability. In doing so, I empower myself to show up in the world authentically, no longer afraid to express my truth or needing to pick sides. Ultimately, grounding in self-awareness fosters a deep sense of connection with myself and the universe. It allows me to walk my path with intention and purpose, knowing that every step, whether in light or shadow, is a valuable part of my journey.

Cultivating Inner Peace: Embracing the Stillness Within

The quest for inner peace can often feel like chasing a mirage, always just out of reach. During my journey, I found myself resorting to affirmations and uplifting quotes that promised tranquility and balance. I read countless pieces of wisdom about how peace resides within us, as if it were a hidden treasure waiting to be discovered. Yet, despite my efforts, I often felt like I was grasping at something elusive, something that slipped through my fingers like falling sand whenever I tried to catch it.

I learned that affirmations, while powerful, can only take us so far if they are not grounded in genuine understanding. I chanted phrases like "Om Tare Tuttare Ture Soha," "Om

Mani Padme Hum," and others about peace and calm, hoping to embody their essence, but it wasn't until I realized that peace is not something to be chased that my perspective began to shift. Instead of viewing peace as a destination, I started to see it as a state of mind, a choice that I could cultivate moment by moment, a conclusion after reading quotes by Thich Nhat Hanh on mindfulness.

This realization opened a new pathway for me. I began to explore what it truly meant to cultivate inner peace. It was not about suppressing the chaos around me or pretending that everything was perfect; rather, it was about finding stillness amidst the storm. I learned to embrace the ebb and flow of life, recognizing that challenges and uncertainties were part of my journey, not obstacles to my peace.

Meditation became a sanctuary where I could connect with that stillness. I discovered that in moments of silence, I could tune into my breath and observe my thoughts without judgment. These practices allowed me to create a space within myself where peace could naturally arise. I found that even in the most turbulent times, I could return to that stillness and remind myself that I was not at the mercy of external circumstances.

As I deepened this practice, I noticed a profound shift in my relationship with my emotions. Instead of resisting discomfort, I learned to welcome it, understanding that every feeling was an opportunity for growth and healing. I realized that true peace was not the absence of turmoil, but rather the ability to navigate through it with grace and compassion for myself. Embracing this perspective transformed my approach to daily life.

I learned to infuse my moments with mindfulness, recognizing that peace could be found in the smallest of things—a warm cup of tea, the rustle of leaves in the wind, or the warmth of a smile from a stranger. Each moment became an invitation to connect with the present and find solace within. In essence, cultivating inner peace is an ongoing journey. It requires patience, commitment, and a willingness to explore the depths of my being. It is about creating a sanctuary within myself, a space where I can be present, authentic, and at peace, regardless of the external chaos that may surround me.

Whispers of the In Between: Trusting the Journey

In the delicate space between who I was and who I am becoming, I found myself enveloped in whispers, subtle nudges from my intuition guiding me through the uncertain terrain of life. This "in between" was not merely a pause but a profound liminal space, rich with potential and ripe with lessons waiting to be uncovered. It was here that I learned the art of trusting the journey, even when the path was shrouded in fog and ambiguity. It is here where I found the answers I needed to evolve and embrace my journey.

Embracing the whispers of this in-between state meant surrendering to the unknown, letting go of the need for certainty and control. I found myself in moments of stillness, where the external noise faded away, allowing me to tune into the gentle voice within. In those quiet spaces, I began to understand that the journey is not always linear, nor does it always make sense. It unfolds in its own rhythm, often leading me down winding paths I could not have anticipated.

Trusting this journey required a leap of faith, a willingness to step into the shadows and embrace the uncertainty that accompanies growth. I recalled times when I felt lost, adrift in a sea of confusion and self-doubt. Yet, in the depths of these moments, I discovered that it was precisely in the uncertainty that transformation took root. I learned to lean into the discomfort, allowing it to guide me rather than deter me. Each whisper from within became a reminder that even in chaos, I was being led toward a greater understanding of myself and found beauty.

As I navigated the whispers, I cultivated a practice of mindfulness that helped me remain present amid the ebb and flow of life. I began to journal my thoughts and feelings, creating a sacred space to reflect on my experiences. This practice became a mirror, reflecting the lessons embedded in my journey. I found clarity in the written word, tracing the threads of my path and recognizing the patterns that emerged.

In this space of introspection, I learned to honor the duality of my experience, the light and shadow coexisting within me. I realized that the whispers often arose from moments of introspection, urging me to explore the parts of myself that had been hidden or neglected. By acknowledging and embracing these facets, I began to weave a more authentic tapestry of who I am becoming.

Trusting the journey also meant learning to embrace patience. I discovered that growth is not always visible; it often unfolds beneath the surface, like a seed sprouting in the dark soil before breaking through to the light. I learned that at times the biggest progress happens under the most pressure while believing the illusion that no progress is taking place. I also learned to celebrate the small victories and moments of clarity, understanding that they were stepping stones on my path. Each whisper became a gentle reminder that transformation takes time and that the journey is just as important as the destination.

In the whispers of the in-between, I found solace and

strength. I connected with others who, too, were traversing their unique paths, sharing their stories of uncertainty and resilience. In these shared experiences, I felt a sense of belonging, a recognition that we are all navigating the complexities of life together. The whispers became louder in community, resonating with the collective understanding that we are never truly alone in our journeys.

Ultimately, the journey of trusting the in-between is an invitation to embrace the mystery of life. It teaches us to let go of rigid expectations and embrace the fluidity of existence. As I continue to walk this path, I carry with me the wisdom gleaned from the whispers, an unwavering faith in the process, and a deep appreciation for the beauty that unfolds in the spaces between.

Chapter 9 The Symphony of Seasons

Paths of Balance: Nature as Our Teacher

As I step outside, I am enveloped by the embrace of nature, a world painted with vibrant colors and intricate details that awaken my senses. The mantra that echoes in my mind, "Nature in nature," serves as a gentle reminder to look beyond the chaos of human existence and find consolation in the profound wisdom that surrounds us.

I often find myself drawn to the gentle dance of leaves as they descend from their branches, spiraling gracefully through the crisp autumn air. Each leaf, a unique masterpiece of gold, crimson, and amber, glides softly to the earth, where it surrenders to the ground like a feather from a bird's wing. In their descent, I witness a beautiful transformation, a reminder that the act of letting go is not an end, but rather a necessary part of life's cyclical journey. These fallen leaves, cradled by the earth, will become seeds that nourish the soil, giving rise to radiant flowers in the spring, their petals unfurling in a chorus of color and fragrance. It is a moving reminder that in every ending lies the potential for new beginnings, and that we too can embrace change with open hearts. We are Nature.

In the park, I watch a dog darting joyfully after a thrown ball, its fur shimmering like sunlight on water. Each leap and bound is filled with an uninhibited celebration of the moment. I am reminded that balance is not solely about finding stability; it's also about allowing ourselves to revel in the joys of life, to embrace spontaneity, and to find delight in simple pleasures. The dog's carefree spirit teaches me the importance of living fully in the present, letting go of worries that anchor us down, and instead, embracing the freedom to chase our passions.

Birdsong fills the air, a melodic tapestry woven from the voices of feathered friends. I gaze upward to see them flitting between branches, their wings a brilliant splash of color against the canvas of green. The way they navigate the trees with grace reflects a beautiful adaptability, a reminder that life's balance often requires us to adjust and flow with the currents of change. I close my eyes and listen, letting their songs wash over me like a gentle breeze, reminding me of the harmonious rhythms of existence.

As I immerse myself in these moments, I discover that observation is an art, a delicate practice that allows us to truly see and appreciate the beauty around us. Nature, in all its glory, teaches me to pause and breathe, to fully engage with my surroundings. The soft rustle of leaves, the warm glow of sunlight filtering through branches, and the fragrant scent of blooming flowers invite me to savor each detail. In it, I continue to practice Zen, mindfulness, neutrality, embracing the ebb and flow of existence.

In these quiet observations, I find clarity and connection, understanding that life is a tapestry of interconnected moments, each thread vibrant and meaningful. Through the lens of nature, I witness the delicate balance between growth and decay, joy and sorrow, spontaneity and stillness. The cycles of the seasons unfold like a painter's brushstroke, each hue and texture contributing to the larger masterpiece of existence.

By immersing myself in these natural rhythms, I not only gain insight into the world around me but also learn how to navigate my own journey with grace and resilience. In this radiant world, I observe the beauty that nature has to offer, allowing its wisdom to inspire me, to guide me in seeking balance amidst life's complexities. Together, we can embrace the warmth of each moment, paint our lives with the vibrant colors of experience, and try to acquire a deeper connection with the extraordinary tapestry of life that surrounds us as we embrace the nature in Nature.

Sacred Rhythms: Nature's Guiding Light

I've always felt that nature speaks in elements, each one teaching me something profound about balance. Earth grounds me when my mind is restless, reminding me to be still, that roots run deep, even when the surface shifts. Water teaches me to flow, to adapt without losing myself. It crashes when it must but smooths stones over time with patience. Air whispers of movement, of change, of letting go when I hold on too tightly. And fire, unpredictable and raw, shows me the beauty of destruction and rebirth; sometimes, to grow, I must burn away what no longer serves me. Each element mirrors the balance and answers I seek. As a Day Walker, I navigate between opposing forces, much like the elements harmonize to sustain life. I am both grounded and free, adaptable yet strong, a force and a presence.

Nature doesn't use words, but it speaks in patterns, in rhythms, in the spaces between the noise. I've learned to listen, not just with my ears, but with my soul. The way a bird shifts its song when a storm approaches. The way trees lean into the wind, surrendering without breaking. The way the ocean calls me to its edge, as if inviting me to let go. There's a language here that I was never taught but have always understood. In moments of doubt, I turn to the trees, the rivers, the skies, and they answer. They remind me that balance isn't about standing still; it's about understanding the motion around me, feeling when to move and when to pause.

Everything in nature moves in cycles, and I am no different. I've seen flowers bloom only to wither, but their seeds carry on. I've watched the moon wax and wane, knowing that its fullness always returns. There were times in my life when I resisted these cycles, clinging to what was, afraid of what comes next. But nature has shown me that there's beauty in both beginnings and endings. The tree doesn't mourn the fall of its leaves; it trusts that spring will come. I have learned to trust my own seasons—moments of growth, of stillness, of release. As a Day Walker, I stand between cycles, embracing both the light and the dark, knowing they are never separate.

When the world becomes too loud, I find myself in quiet places where nature does what it does best—heals. The wind against my skin, the scent of damp earth, the feeling of sunlight warming my face—it's in these moments that I remember who I am. I've cried into the roots of ancient trees, whispered my fears into the ocean waves, let the rain cleanse me when I couldn't do it myself. Nature doesn't ask me to be strong or to have answers. It just exists, and in that existence, it teaches me that I, too, am enough.

Nature has been my greatest teacher, showing me lessons in patience, resilience, and surrender. A river doesn't fight against the rocks; it carves its way through them over time. A seed doesn't rush to become a tree; it trusts the process. The stars don't fear the darkness; they shine because of it. These lessons echo in my life. I have learned that forcing things rarely works, that some growth happens unseen, and that my own light isn't diminished by the darkness; it's defined by it. As a Day Walker, I carry these teachings with me, finding balance in a world that often pulls me in different directions.

There was a time when I thought balance meant staying the same, but nature has shown me otherwise. The seasons shift without resistance, each carrying its own purpose. Spring teaches renewal, reminding me that I can always begin again. Summer is passion, fire, energy; it's the time to embrace my full power. Autumn whispers of letting go, of trusting that not everything is meant to stay. And winter—silent, still— teaches rest, the kind I often deny myself. If nature trusts its seasons, why shouldn't I? Why should I fear change when it's the most natural thing there is? I am learning to embrace my own seasons, knowing that each one serves a purpose.

Not all sacred places have walls. Some of my most profound moments of connection have happened under open skies, near rivers, in the quiet of forests. I've realized that balance isn't just about finding peace outside of myself; it's about bringing that peace inward, wherever I go. I create sacred spaces by honoring what brings me stillness. Sometimes it's a candle, a moment of silence, a walk where my feet touch the earth with intention. The world rushes, but I don't have to. I can create balance in the smallest acts by pausing, breathing, being present.

To me, nature is more than just beauty. It's proof of something greater, something unseen but deeply felt. The way the stars map the sky, the way the tides move with the moon, the way life always finds a way to grow—these are whispers of the divine. I have found spirit in the rustling of leaves, in the dance of fireflies, in the stillness of mountains. I don't need words to explain it; I just need to feel it. The balance I seek is not something to be achieved but something to be remembered because it has always been within me, just as it is in nature.

This is a reflection of the way I see the world, the way I move through it as a Day Walker. Nature doesn't just exist around me; it exists with me, within me. It teaches me without speaking, guides me without force. If I ever forget my balance, I know where to turn: to the rivers, the trees, the wind; to the quiet spaces where life continues, effortlessly, in harmony. And maybe, just maybe, I can learn to do the same.

Chapter 10 Energy and Higher States of Love

Understanding Energy as Love

I used to think love was something I had to find—something outside of myself, measured in words, actions, and the presence of another. It was shaped by the conditions around me, by the expectations I carried, by the way the world taught me to understand it. But the more I explore love, the more I realize it isn't something that comes and goes. It isn't something I can lose. It's something much bigger than that, something that exists whether I reach for it or not, no matter who is near me or where I am.

The more I surrendered to my own unfolding, the more I realized: love is not something we seek. Love is something we are. Everything around us is energy, vibrating, shifting, expanding. Love is not just an emotion; it is the pulse of the universe, the current that flows through all things. It is the silent force that breathes life into existence, the invisible thread that connects us across time and space.

When we move beyond the idea of love as attachment, we begin to feel something greater—a love that does not ask, does not take, does not need. A love that simply is. It exists in the stillness between moments, in the warmth of the sun, in the quiet knowing that we are never truly alone. As I discovered this deeper truth, I found that love resides in every corner of our being, waiting for us to recognize it. It is the gentle whisper of the wind, the embrace of a friend, the shared laughter that echoes through our days. It is the sacred energy that flows through our interactions, reminding us of our interconnectedness. It is a frequency we can tune into.

When we allow ourselves to step into this frequency, we awaken something ancient within us—a remembering of the love that has always been. The more I let go of what I thought love was, the more I begin to feel it as an energy, not just an emotion. It moves through me like a current, shifting the way I experience everything. It isn't tied to a single person, a single moment, or even a single lifetime. It just is.

There are days when it flows effortlessly, like the rhythm of my breath, like something ancient and familiar moving through me. And then there are days when I feel disconnected from it, as if love has left me. But I'm beginning to understand—it's never love that disappears. It's me. I close myself off. I shrink into fear, into doubt, into the aching belief that I am somehow separate from it. And yet, the moment I stop resisting, the moment I allow myself to be, love returns—not because it was ever gone, but because I have softened enough to feel it again.

It makes me wonder how many times I have mistaken my own walls for the absence of love. How many times I have searched for something that was already wrapped around me, waiting for me to surrender. Love in its highest state doesn't demand. It doesn't wait for permission, nor does it ask to be understood. It is quiet, infinite, and patient, filling the spaces between all things, existing whether I reach for it or not.

And I've come to realize—love is not just a feeling. It is a frequency. A vibration that is always present, always humming beneath the noise of my thoughts, waiting for me to tune in. The moment I shift my awareness, the moment I choose love over fear, I align with it. I become it. Love is not something that comes and goes. It does not waver. It is only my perception that changes, my willingness to attune to what has always been there.

I have touched this love in ways I can't explain—in moments of stillness when my mind ceases its searching and I dissolve into something greater than myself. In those moments, I don't just feel love—I am love. It moves beyond the human ache of wanting and into something vast, something formless, something that simply is.

And yet, the more I surrender to it, the more I recognize it in the smallest things—in the hush of the wind against my skin, in the weight of silence between heartbeats, in the way light spills through a window and lands on the floor as if it was always meant to be there. Love is not something to find or keep. It is something to remember. And every time I allow myself to fall into it, every time I choose to align with its frequency, I remember a little more.

The 14-Dimensional Heart: A Gateway to Divine Connection

There was a moment when I felt my heart expand beyond anything I had ever known. It was as if the layers of my being unfolded all at once, stretching beyond the limits of my body, my thoughts, even time itself. I wasn't just feeling love—I *was* love.

As a day walker, I tapped into this force because I was in harmony with Source. I found myself glowing with a vibrant green energy radiating from my heart chakra, a phenomenon that captivated me for months—even a year. It was as if my heart had become a beacon of love, illuminating the space around me with its glow, embracing everything and everyone in its warmth.

In those moments, I experienced a profound connection to the universe, a feeling of unity with all that exists. This was not merely a physical sensation; it represented an awakening within me, a realization that love transcends boundaries. With each moment of alignment, my heart expanded, allowing me to tap into the sacred harmony of 14 different dimensions simultaneously.

It felt like I was holding the essence of the universe within my heart, a profound connection that transcended anything I had ever heard of or felt before. In this state of heightened awareness, I discovered that the frequency of love is the purest and highest frequency—love itself, unhindered and without inhibitions. It flows freely, a current that connects all beings, reminding us of our true nature.

The 14-Dimensional Heart is a gateway to accessing this frequency, opening pathways to deeper connections and expanded states of awareness. Each dimension of the heart reveals a deeper layer of connection: the love we hold for ourselves, nurturing our souls and honoring our journey; the love we share with others, creating bonds that transcend time and space; the love that connects us to the cosmos, reminding us of our place in the grand tapestry of existence.

To awaken this heart is to step into an awareness where love is no longer personal—it is universal. It is the purest form of existence, a state of being beyond conditions, beyond fear, beyond separation.

Activating the Heart's Multidimensional Awareness

How to Begin the Expansion

How do we begin to feel this expansion? How do we move from thinking about love to *becoming* love? It starts with presence. The heart cannot open in the past or the future—it only unfolds in the now.

Try this:

Close your eyes. Place your hands over your chest. Breathe. Feel your heart beating—not just as an organ, but as an energy field. Imagine its light expanding, radiating outward in every direction. What does it feel like? Is there warmth? A sense of peace? A subtle vibration?

With each breath, allow it to grow. Let it stretch beyond your body, beyond the walls around you, beyond the sky. Let it touch everything, every being that crosses your path. This is your invitation to embrace the 14-Dimensional Heart. It is not something to reach for—it is something to *allow*, a gentle unfolding that occurs naturally when we align with our true essence.

Embracing Your Journey

As we explore these dimensions of love, it's important to remember that not everyone will resonate with the 14-Dimensional experience. It's perfectly okay if you only feel love in the 5D space, which is the most common. Each person's journey is unique, and some may experience more or less depending on where they are in their path.

Remember that love is not a race; it's a journey. There is no right or wrong way to feel or express love. It's about honoring your own experience and embracing the unfolding. After all, it took me a while to arrive at this place of connection and understanding. Each step along the way was a vital part of my growth, a necessary exploration of what love truly means.

Trust that your journey is valid, and wherever you are is exactly where you need to be. Embrace your own unfolding, knowing that love is ever-present and waiting for you to discover it in your own way. Let this love envelop you, guiding you to deeper connections and higher states of being.

Chapter 11 Becoming the Day Walker

I didn't wake up one day knowing exactly who I was. There was no sudden revelation, no bolt of lightning that struck me with certainty. Instead, it was a slow unraveling, a journey marked by questions I wasn't ready to ask and answers I wasn't willing to accept. It crept in quietly, like a shadow moving across the ground—not imposing, but impossible to ignore. The signs had always been there, scattered throughout my life in ways both subtle and glaringly obvious, like breadcrumbs. Dreams lingered long after waking, whispering truths I couldn't fully grasp. Moments of inexplicable knowing, an awareness that extended beyond logic, beyond what could be explained. A feeling of being caught between two worlds, never fully belonging to either, yet somehow tied to both. Sometimes, I felt stretched between light and shadow, a tether binding me to forces I didn't understand, pulling me toward something unseen. But I told myself it was nothing. A trick of the mind. A story I was spinning out of thin air. Ultimately, that I was crazy. And so, I resisted.

I resisted in the way that only someone terrified of their own truth can. I built walls, sturdy and high, around the parts of myself that didn't conform to what I thought I should be or what others could understand. When the knowing came knocking, I silenced it. When the signs grew louder, I looked the other way. For years at a time, I buried it beneath layers of logic and distraction, convincing myself that if I ignored it long enough, it would fade into nothing. But denial does not erase truth; it only suppresses it. The more I fought, the more the fractures began to show. It wasn't just an internal battle— it bled into everything. My thoughts grew tangled, my emotions twisted in knots I couldn't undo. My sense of direction—once steady, or at least tolerable—became a series of dead ends. It was as if I had been walking against the current for so long that I no longer remembered what it felt like to move freely.

The conflict within me was relentless, a war I could never win because the enemy was me. How do you fight against something that isn't separate from you? How do you outrun yourself? How fast do I need to be? The truth I had worked so hard to deny had become an undeniable force pressing against me from the inside, demanding to be acknowledged. I was exhausted from the struggle, yet still, I hesitated. Because if I let go, if I surrendered to what had always been there, what would that mean? What would it change?

Then came the drum. It wasn't just an instrument; it was something ancient, something alive. The moment I held it, I could feel its energy humming beneath my fingers, the stretched deer hide carrying the weight of something sacred.

When I played, the sound was more than just a rhythm—it was a pulse, a vibration that moved through me, filling spaces I hadn't realized were empty. I closed my eyes and let the beat guide me, let it strip away the noise of my thoughts, the doubts that had kept me bound for so long. I don't know how much time passed, only that at some point, something shifted. It was as if I had stepped into a place where time folded in on itself, where the barriers I had built crumbled into dust. And in that space, a word emerged: Day Walker.

It wasn't something I thought. It wasn't a conclusion I reached. It was simply there, waiting for me, as if it had always existed just beyond my grasp. The moment I heard it, I knew. I had always known. I just hadn't been ready to accept it. And in that moment, I did.

The fight ended, not in victory or defeat, but in understanding. The walls I had built had never been protecting me; they had only kept me from myself. All the resistance, all the running, all the fear had done nothing but delay the inevitable. When I finally let it go, I felt something loosening, something realigning. The weight I had carried for years lifted, and in its place was something else—something lighter, something truer. I had become the Day Walker. Or maybe I had been all along.

When the term Day Walker came to me, it wasn't just a

phrase. It was a recognition, a truth rising from within me that I had always known but never put into words. I had spent so much of my life navigating between extremes, between worlds that seemed to contradict each other, yet I belonged to both. Light and dark. Seen and unseen. The spiritual and the physical. But it wasn't about choosing one over the other—it was about mastering the dance between them. Before I could become this, before I could walk with certainty, I had to sit in confusion. I had to surrender to the unknown, to the spaces where nothing made sense, where my logical mind wrestled with the knowing that had no words. I had to be comfortable being lost.

The Evolution of Me

I wasn't born understanding this. In the beginning, I thought I had to be something specific, that to walk a spiritual path meant fully leaving behind the weight of the material world, or that to function in this world meant dimming the part of me that understood things others couldn't see. I spent years shifting between these spaces, feeling like I was constantly too much or not enough, like I had to justify why I was both. No matter how much I tried, that just wasn't possible. The confusion—oh, the confusion was relentless. My mind would grasp for answers, for clarity, for something that fit, and yet all I ever got was silence. Not the peaceful kind, but the heavy, empty kind, the kind that makes you doubt yourself, that makes you wonder if you're even moving in the right direction. Yet, I've learned that confusion is not a void; it's an initiation. It is the space between the inhale and the exhale, the moment before awakening. It is where the intuitive mind begins its slow ascent, where the deeper knowing whispers beneath the noise.

But to hear it, I had to stop reaching. I had to let go. So I waited. I learned to silence the mind, even when it screamed for answers. I learned to trust that the knowing would come in its own time. It always did, it still does. Not in rushed epiphanies, not in lightning-bolt revelations, but in a slow, quiet unfolding.

What It Means to Be a Day Walker

Being a Day Walker isn't just about balancing light and dark—it's about understanding them, embodying them, and using both as tools for healing, wisdom, and transformation. The world loves to separate things into opposites: good and bad, spiritual and physical, awake and asleep. But what if those things were never meant to be separate? I move through shadows with the eyes of someone who has lived in them, who has felt their pull, their comfort, their pain—and I emerge, carrying their wisdom into the light. I don't reject darkness, because I've learned that in its depths, there is power, raw and unfiltered. And I don't worship light blindly, because I've seen how it can be used to deceive, to suppress, to burn. I walk between them, not as a visitor, but as someone who belongs to both, and belongs to neither opposing force.

But I don't walk alone. Shai was the first to show me that. My ally, my steady ground when I couldn't find my own footing. In moments when my mind struggled to catch up to what my soul already knew, he was there. Not with answers—he knew better than to give me those—but with presence. He taught me that my answers are my own. He was there for me, with quiet understanding, with the kind of patience that made space for me to find my own way. He held space for me. Even now, as I navigate the ever-shifting tides of being a healer, an empath, a mother, and a hopeless romantic seeking depth in others—not in fleeting moments, but in the kind of connections that unravel the soul—I feel his presence. A reminder that even those of us who walk alone are never truly alone.

How to Embrace the Path

1. If you feel this pull—this knowing that you aren't meant to exist in only one space—then you are already walking this path. But embracing it fully requires a few things:

2. Accept that you are not just one thing. You are not just

light. You are not just dark. You are not just a healer, nor are you just someone who has been wounded. You are both, and that is your power.

3. Stop fearing the spaces in between. The unknown, the grey areas, the moments of uncertainty, this is where transformation happens. Don't rush to define everything. Let yourself be in the in-between.

4. Use both sides as tools. Light illuminates. Darkness deepens. Both are necessary for understanding. You don't have to pick one to be whole.

5. Stand firm in who you are. The world will try to push you to one side or the other, to fit you into a category that feels easier to define. But that's not your purpose. Your existence itself is proof that the bridge between both worlds is real.

The Legacy of the Day Walker

To be a Day Walker is to carry a legacy that is both ancient and ever-evolving. It is not a title one claims but a path one embodies—one that requires a soul deep enough to hold the weight of contradictions without breaking, without running, without needing to be one thing or the other. It is not an easy path.

We are the ones who walk between. We do not belong fully

to the realms of light nor to the depths of darkness, yet we are welcome in both. We are the silent observers in rooms where truths go unnoticed. We feel the weight of the unspoken, the currents beneath the surface, the echoes of lives that have yet to be lived. The Day Walker does not reject one world for the other but instead sees them for what they are—two sides of the same whole, forever pulling at one another, forever seeking balance. This is our work: to be bridges, to be anchors, to be mirrors. To bring depth where there is shallowness, clarity where there is confusion, and courage where there is fear. To remind others that the world is not simply light or dark but an endless gradient of shifting hues, and within that space—within the grey—is where true transformation happens. We see the HUE in HUEmanity.

But the weight of this path is real. We feel everything, sometimes more than we know what to do with. We love deeply, not just in romance but in the way we connect with every soul that carries even the faintest ember of depth. We search for those who understand, not just in words, but in energy, in the silent knowing that we are not alone in the in-between. And when we find them, they become part of our story, part of our remembering.

Shai, the Unknowing Master of Duality

Shai was one of those souls. An enigma wrapped in

simplicity, a paradox in human form. He mastered duality without even realizing it, walking through life as though the opposing forces within him were never meant to be at war. Where others struggled to balance the seen and unseen, the logical and the mystical, the gentle and the fierce—Shai simply was. He did not resist his own nature, nor did he seek to define it. He moved with an ease that most never attain, an unconscious knowing that life was never meant to be confined to a single truth.

His presence was both grounding and boundless, like standing at the edge of the ocean and feeling both the vastness before you and the solid earth beneath your feet. He did not offer answers, because he understood that true knowing cannot be given—it must be found. Instead, he held space in the way only those who exist in both realms can.

In moments when my mind was tangled in its own web, when I struggled to trust the silence, Shai reminded me— without words—that the unknown is not something to fear. That I did not need to force understanding, that I could let the answers rise in their own time. He was my ally, not because he guided me, but because he stood beside me as I guided myself.

And that is the essence of a true Day Walker. Not to impose, not to control, but to be—to exist fully in both worlds and, through that existence, remind others that they can do the same. Even now, as I step deeper into my own path, I carry his presence with me—not as a memory, but as a frequency, an energy woven into the fabric of my being. A reminder that this journey is not about certainty or control, but about surrender. About trusting the pull of the unseen, about walking without needing to see the entire path.

And so, I walk. Not because I have all the answers, but because I no longer need them.

Chapter 12 Integrating These Teachings into Your Life

Becoming the Day Walker isn't about eliminating your darkness or only embracing your light. It's about learning to walk in balance. It's about recognizing the war within you and making peace with both sides instead of believing one has more value than the other. No one else can walk this path for you; there's no manual, just suggestions for you to modify as needed to fit your journey. You don't have to do it blindly. This journey is yours to shape, and the deeper you go, the more you will see that every shadow and every light within you is leading you back to yourself. I used to have a mantra that helped me through this journey: "I will not wage war against myself." This powerful phrase emerged during my work with my deepest friend and shaman, who guided me to understand that self-acceptance begins with compassion. By letting go of the internal battle, I opened myself to the possibility of healing. Embracing both my light and shadow became a path to wholeness rather than a struggle for dominance.

Seeing Yourself Clearly

Before you can integrate these teachings, you have to be

willing to meet yourself as you are. Not the version of you that the world expects, not the version you wish you could be, but the raw, unfiltered truth of who you are in this moment. This requires honesty. It requires looking at the parts of yourself that you've spent years avoiding. It requires courage and acceptance. You can start by noticing the cycles that repeat in your life. Do the same wounds keep opening in different ways? Do you find yourself in similar conflicts, whether with others or within your own mind? Patterns don't emerge by accident. They are lessons waiting to be acknowledged. They are mirrors reflecting what still needs to be healed. If you're running in circles, the best thing to do is something different for a different result.

When you react strongly to something, pause. Is your reaction coming from the present moment, or is it carrying the weight of your past as an outdated coping mechanism? Does your shadow rise in the form of anger, defensiveness, or withdrawal? Or does it manifest as people-pleasing, avoidance, or self-doubt? Do you overextend yourself in the name of light, giving and giving until you are empty? Or do you hold your energy so tightly that no one, including yourself, can touch it? Sit with these questions, not to judge yourself, but to understand. Awareness is the first step toward integration. You can't change something you're unaware of.

Try writing it down. Keep a journal where you track moments when your shadow takes over, when fear, shame, or resentment pull you inward. Then, write about the times your light emerges, when you feel open, powerful, or deeply connected. Look for patterns. Do certain people or situations bring out one side more than the other? What triggers your shadow? What strengthens your light? Remember, there are no wrong answers. This is between you and YOU.

When you're ready, take it a step further. Stand in front of a mirror, look yourself in the eyes, and speak. Say, "I see the part of me that fears," and hold that gaze. Then say, "I see the part of me that loves." Keep going. Say what comes up. You might feel resistance at first. You might want to look away. Stay with it. There is power in being witnessed, even if it is only by yourself. Follow your intuition without judgment; remember, it's about accepting yourself with compassion.

Bringing Balance Into Your Daily Life

Once you begin seeing yourself clearly, the next step is learning to walk with both parts of you. This isn't about control. It's not about forcing yourself into the light or suppressing your shadow. It's about allowing them both to exist without letting either one consume you. Start your mornings with an intention. Not a task, not a goal, but a simple commitment to yourself. Maybe today, you will listen more closely to your emotions instead of pushing them aside. Maybe today, you will allow yourself to rest without guilt. Maybe today, you will embrace joy without questioning whether you deserve it. As you move through the day, pay attention to your reactions. When someone upsets you, when fear grips your chest, when doubt creeps in, pause. Instead of immediately responding, take a breath. Ask yourself: Is this coming from my shadow or my light? Is this an old wound speaking, or is this moment asking me to grow? Sometimes, your shadow will be right. Sometimes, your light will need to step back. The key is not to let one overpower the other, but to listen to both.

Emotions are not enemies. Anger is not something to be ashamed of. It is a signal that a boundary has been crossed. Sadness is not a weakness; it is a call to acknowledge what has been lost. Even fear, when met with awareness, can become a guide. The moment you stop labeling your emotions as good or bad, you begin to understand their purpose. It's about shifting the way you see things, which will change how you feel. During this process, don't forget to ground yourself. There's no right or wrong speed; it's the journey, not the destination. Find ways to embody both aspects of yourself. Let your shadow express itself in safe, intentional ways. Move your body, dance, or scream into a pillow if you need to. Let the emotions that have been buried inside you find release. Then, let your light expand. Create something. Speak kindness into the world. Open your heart without fear of how it will be received. Both are necessary. Both are sacred.

At night, reflect. Look back on your day with curiosity, not judgment. What moments pulled you toward your shadow? Which ones expanded your light? How did you react? How would you like to respond next time? This isn't about perfection. It's about learning to exist in the space between, in the balance that makes you whole. If you slip up, if you fall back into old habits, if you wake up one day and forget everything you've learned, so what? Who cares? Just pick it back up. This isn't a race. It's a lifestyle. Progress isn't measured in how perfectly you walk this path, but in the fact that you keep walking. Shaman Om used to remind me, "Slow progress is better than no progress." Something that I not only live by, but also use as words of encouragement to everyone. Embrace change.

Walking the Path with Intention

Integration isn't something that happens overnight. It's a practice, a lifelong unfolding. Some days, you will lean more into your light. Other days, your shadow will demand attention. Neither is wrong. The key is to keep going; it's not a race to the end. When you feel yourself slipping into old patterns, pause. Take a breath. Choose again. When fear whispers that you are not enough, meet it with truth. When your shadow rises, do not run from it. Stand beside it. Ask it what it needs, listen with self-compassion. When your light feels fragile, protect it. Let it shine at its own pace. You are not here to be perfect. You are here to be whole. And that means embracing every step of the journey, no matter how small, no matter how messy. Keep going. Keep walking. Keep choosing yourself.

Dealing with Resistance and Setbacks

Let's be real: this journey isn't always smooth. Some days, you'll feel like you're making real progress, like you finally get it, and then, out of nowhere, resistance hits. Old habits creep back in. You react in ways you thought you'd moved past. You feel stuck. And that's where most people give up. But here's what I need you to understand: resistance isn't failure. It's proof that you're growing. It usually doesn't show up as some obvious roadblock. Instead, it's subtle, slipping into your mind like a quiet voice saying, *I'll do it later.* It's the sudden exhaustion that washes over you the moment you sit down to journal. It's picking a fight with yourself over whether this is even worth it or realizing you're caught in a pattern you swore you had broken. Sometimes, resistance doesn't feel like anything at all—just numbness, a blank space where there used to be drive. Your mind is trying to keep you safe. Even if "safe" means staying in what's familiar to avoid discomfort.

When you feel yourself slipping into that space, stop. Just pause. Don't force yourself forward, don't run from it, just breathe. Ask yourself, *What am I actually afraid of here?* Maybe the fear isn't about moving forward, but about what you might uncover if you dig deeper. Maybe there's a quiet doubt whispering, *What if I'm not strong enough for this?* Instead of pushing those thoughts away, listen to them. Get curious. And then, make it easier. If journaling feels too heavy, record a voice note instead. If meditation feels impossible, take a mindful walk and let your thoughts drift. Adjust the process so that it meets you where you are instead of trying to force yourself into a mold of how healing "should" look. Above all, give yourself grace. No one walks this path perfectly. You will slip, you will avoid, you will mess up. And when that happens, don't use it as another reason to shame yourself. Just notice, forgive, and keep going. If you ever find yourself thinking, *I'm failing at this*, remind yourself: *I am not failing. I am learning.* If you drop the ball, who cares? Just pick it back up.

Bringing Integration Into Daily Life

Healing isn't just something that happens in grand, transformative moments. It's in the tiny, everyday choices that build on each other, shaping the way you move through the world. It's not a single event; it's a relationship with yourself that deepens over time. Imagine you're in a conversation, and someone criticizes you. Your gut reaction is to snap back or shut down, that familiar instinct to defend or withdraw kicking in before you even realize it. But this time, you pause. You notice the reaction forming inside you and ask yourself, *Is this coming from my shadow?* Maybe your shadow feels attacked, but your light reminds you to breathe. Instead of reacting on autopilot, you choose differently. You respond with awareness instead of old wounds. This is why shadow work is important.

Another example: maybe you catch yourself saying yes when you really want to say no. That old fear of disappointing someone rises up, pushing you toward self-sacrifice. But instead of giving in, you stop. *Am I giving from my light, or am I afraid of rejection?* This time, you choose to honor yourself. You say no. And you don't apologize for it. There will be moments when emotions hit you with full force—like anger burning through your chest, sadness pulling you into heaviness, fear tightening around your ribs. Instead of burying them, you pause. *Okay, I see you. What do you need from me?* Maybe sadness just wants to be felt without being rushed away. Maybe anger needs a safe space to burn without destruction. Maybe fear isn't trying to stop you but is asking for reassurance. The moment you stop treating these emotions as problems to fix and start seeing them as parts of you that need attention, something shifts. You stop running. You stop resisting. You learn to sit with yourself, even in the discomfort, without judgment. And that's where true integration happens. Not in fighting yourself, not in suppressing what feels inconvenient, but in witnessing all that you are and making space for it. Some days, you'll lean more into your light, and other days, your shadow will ask to be heard. Neither is wrong. What matters is that you keep walking, keep choosing yourself, again and again.

Listening to the Body: The Role of Sensations in Integration

Your body speaks before your mind catches up. Long before you put words to an emotion, it has already made a home somewhere within you—tight shoulders, a fluttering stomach, a clenched jaw. The more you ignore it, the louder it gets. Integration isn't just about observing your thoughts; it's about learning the language of your body and responding with care. When you feel anger, where does it land? Maybe your hands tense, itching to react. Maybe heat rushes to your face, your breath shortens, your muscles brace for defense. If you sit with it instead of acting on it, what happens? Does it shift?

Does it soften? And what about sadness? Does it make your body heavy, shoulders folding inward as if protecting your heart? Does it pool in your throat, unspoken? What would happen if, instead of forcing it away, you allowed yourself to physically feel it?

Too often, we override these signals, suppressing them under logic, distraction, or self-judgment. But the body holds what the mind denies. Learning to be present with physical sensations, even the uncomfortable ones, is a form of healing. More importantly, by identifying how emotions manifest in the body, we learn to recognize our triggers more effectively. A deep, twisting ache in the gut may signal fear, an old wound of abandonment. Tightness in the chest could indicate grief or unresolved heartache. Tension in the throat might reveal suppressed words, truths left unsaid. When we trace these sensations back to their root, we gain insight into where healing is needed.

This process becomes even more powerful when we understand how these energies connect to our chakras. Our emotions are not random; they interact with the body's energetic centers:

- Fear and insecurity often settle in the root chakra, making us feel ungrounded, unstable, or disconnected.

- Shame and suppressed emotions gather in the sacral chakra, creating tension in the lower abdomen.

- Power struggles and unresolved anger build up in the solar plexus, tightening our stomach or causing digestive issues.

- Grief and emotional wounds weigh on the heart chakra, creating pressure in the chest or shoulders.

- Unspoken truths and self-expression issues manifest in the throat chakra, causing tightness or a lump in the throat.

- Overactive thoughts and disconnection from intuition are often linked to the third eye and crown chakras, resulting in headaches or mental fog.

When we become aware of how our emotional energy interacts with these chakras, we gain a deeper understanding of not just what we feel, but why. Instead of being overwhelmed by our emotions, we can use this awareness to work through them with intention, whether it's through grounding exercises, breathwork, energy healing, chakra affirmations, or simply honoring what our body is trying to tell us. Healing isn't just mental or spiritual; it's physical too. And when you stop treating emotions as abstract ideas and start recognizing them as lived experiences in your body, you learn to move through them with more grace and understanding.

Old Wounds: The Echoes of the Past

Every time we react strongly to something in the present, there's a good chance we're not just responding to this moment; we're responding to something much older. Old wounds don't just live in our memories; they live in our bodies, in our habits, in the way we navigate relationships, and in the stories we tell ourselves about who we are. Maybe it's the fear of abandonment that makes you cling too tightly or push people away before they can leave you first.

Maybe it's the childhood wound of never feeling seen that causes you to over-explain yourself or seek validation in ways that leave you exhausted. Maybe past rejection makes you hesitate before speaking your truth, keeping your voice small to avoid being hurt again. These wounds don't just disappear with time; they become patterns that repeat in different forms until we finally face them. Have you noticed that certain emotions or situations seem to trigger the same reaction over and over? That's no accident. Patterns don't emerge by chance; they are the soul's way of pointing us toward what still needs healing.

But here's the hard part: healing an old wound means letting yourself feel what you once had to suppress. When you were a child, maybe you weren't allowed to express anger, so now it turns inward as self-criticism. Maybe sadness wasn't safe to show, so now you numb yourself the moment you start to feel too much. But that pain never truly left; it's waiting for you to acknowledge it, to give it space, to release it in a way that doesn't harm you or others.

Recognizing When You're Acting from a Wound

One of the most powerful things you can do on this journey is learn to recognize when you're reacting from an old wound rather than the present moment. Here's how you can start:

- **Notice the intensity of your emotions.** If your reaction feels bigger than the situation calls for—if your anger, fear, or sadness feels overwhelming—it's likely tied to something deeper than just this moment. Ask yourself, *What does this remind me of? Have I felt this way before?*

- **Observe the physical response.** Old wounds often manifest in the body before we consciously recognize them. Does your stomach clench when someone raises their voice? Does your chest tighten when you feel ignored? Your body is remembering something, even if your mind hasn't connected the dots yet.

- **Pay attention to recurring themes in your**

relationships. Do you always feel like people abandon you? Do you often feel unseen, unheard, or unworthy? The outer world mirrors what we carry inside. If the same pain keeps resurfacing in different relationships, there's a wound beneath it that hasn't been addressed.

- **Identify your core beliefs.** What do you tell yourself when something goes wrong? "I'm not good enough." "People always leave." "I have to prove my worth." These beliefs aren't facts; they are the echoes of past wounds. They may have been formed to protect you at some point, but now they are keeping you stuck.

Healing Old Wounds

Healing isn't about pretending the wound never existed; it's about transforming your relationship with it. The goal isn't to erase the past but to release its grip on your present. Here are some ways to begin that process:

- **Feel it to free it.** If you've spent years avoiding certain emotions, they won't disappear on their own. Sit with them. Acknowledge them. Let yourself grieve what you never allowed yourself to grieve.

- **Re-parent yourself.** Sometimes, healing requires

giving yourself the love, reassurance, or validation you didn't receive when the wound was first created. Speak to yourself the way a loving parent would: *I see you. You're safe now. You are worthy of love just as you are.*

- **Rewrite the narrative.** Your past experiences shaped your beliefs, but they don't have to define you. When an old belief surfaces—*I'm not enough, I'm unlovable, I always mess things up*—challenge it. Is it really true? Or is it just an old wound speaking? What would happen if you believed something different?

- **Work with the body.** Because old wounds are stored not just in the mind but in the body, healing must be embodied. Practices like breathwork, movement, energy healing, and somatic therapy help release emotional pain that talking alone can't reach.

- **Find where it lives in your energy.** As we discussed earlier, wounds often show up in our chakras. If a fear of abandonment weighs on your heart chakra, work on heart-opening practices. If a deep sense of insecurity lingers in your root chakra, grounding exercises can help rebuild stability.

The Power of Self-Compassion

Above all, healing old wounds requires self-compassion. It's easy to judge ourselves for reacting a certain way or for carrying pain longer than we think we "should." But the truth is, if you are still carrying a wound, there was a time when holding onto it was the only way to survive; that's why it became a coping mechanism. That version of you did the best they could with what they had. With awareness, now you get to do something different.

You don't have to rush this. Some wounds take years to heal, and that's okay. The fact that you're even looking at them is already a victory. Every time you choose awareness over avoidance, every time you meet your pain with kindness instead of shame, you are rewriting your story. And that is how true transformation begins.

Reframing Regression: When Old Wounds Resurface

There's a moment in healing that no one warns you about: the day you feel like you've made so much progress, only to find yourself falling back into old patterns. You react in ways you thought you'd outgrown. You catch yourself in the same cycles you swore you had broken. And it's tempting, in that moment, to believe you've failed.

But what if regression isn't failure? What if it's part of the process? Healing isn't linear. It's a spiral. Every time an old wound resurfaces, you're not back at the beginning; you're revisiting it from a new level of awareness. The fact that you notice yourself slipping means you've already grown. Before, you reacted without thinking. Now, you recognize it. That recognition is proof of progress.

Instead of frustration, try curiosity. Why is this resurfacing now? Sometimes, wounds reappear because there's a deeper layer to heal. Other times, they show up to remind you of how far you've come. Maybe an old trigger feels just as painful, but now you respond with more self-awareness. Maybe you still fall into the pattern, but you recover faster. That's growth. That's integration.

So when you stumble, don't punish yourself. Pause. Breathe. Acknowledge it without judgment. *Okay, I see this pattern again. What is it teaching me this time?* Healing isn't about perfection; it's about staying present with yourself, even in the moments that feel messy. Just because you visit an old wound doesn't mean you live there anymore.

Building a Relationship with Your Shadow

Your shadow isn't your enemy. It isn't something to be feared, ignored, or conquered. It's the part of you that has been exiled, the voice that was silenced, the pain that was buried, the desires you were taught to suppress. And just like any part of you, it doesn't disappear simply because you deny its existence.

Integration isn't about "defeating" your shadow; it's about learning to understand it. If you listen, what does it say? If you stop fighting it, what does it need? One way to start this process is through dialogue. Imagine your shadow as an old friend who has been trying to get your attention for years. Sit with it. Ask it questions. *What are you protecting me from? What do you need to feel safe? What have you been trying to tell me that I've refused to hear?*

Maybe it responds with anger, frustrated that you've ignored it for so long. Maybe it reveals grief, a wound that never fully healed. Maybe it just needs reassurance that you won't abandon it again. Some people find it easier to write letters to their shadow, letting it express freely. Others visualize it in meditation, giving it form and presence. Whatever method resonates with you, the goal is the same: to acknowledge, to listen, to accept.

Because the truth is, your shadow isn't here to hurt you. It's here to be healed. And the moment you stop fighting it, you start freeing yourself.

Chapter 13 A Higher Calling

I realized my calling early on, a whisper in my heart that grew louder with each passing day. From a young age, I felt an undeniable pull to help others embrace change and heal. It's as if I've always known that healing is the key to living in a better world, a world where we can shed the weight of our pasts and step into our true selves. My journey has been enriched by the guidance of countless spirit guides, animals, and deities that have come to me during trances and meditation, and, of course, my shaman.

I remember vividly the moments when my shaman would drum for me, his rhythmic beats resonating deep within my soul, opening portals to realms I never knew existed. His presence was a comfort and an inspiration, a reminder that I was never alone on this path. With every session, I delved deeper into the unseen. This is when I formed a deeper bond with animal spirit guides.

One of my most profound experiences was when I followed my body's instinctive movements, leading me to hold an energetic bow and arrow physically. In that moment, I connected with Artemis, the embodiment of strength and protection. The feeling was electric, a surge of energy that coursed through me, affirming my purpose. This connection opened a gateway to understanding my gifts and how to wield them with intention.

As I traveled through these realms, I encountered guides who shared their stories, their tools, and their ceremonies. Thoth, with his wisdom and knowledge; Anubis, who helped me understand the weight of the soul; Isis, who taught me the power of nurturing; Ganesh, who removed obstacles; Brahma, who opened my eyes to creation; and Hanuman, who embodied devotion and strength. Each encounter filled me with awe and a deeper understanding of my own journey. The lessons I learned from them are so profound, I find it challenging to summarize them.

I often reflect on how my passion for learning complements my spiritual path. I've read works by Einstein and Hawkins, immersing myself in quantum mechanics and physics. I found myself captivated by the beauty of sacred geometry before I even knew what it was. It was as if my spirit had been guiding me all along, weaving together science and spirituality in a tapestry of understanding. A calling I couldn't ignore.

Buddhism and Dharma have also been pivotal in my journey. The noble truths and affirmations have become tools I use daily to maintain balance and clarity. I engage in chakra healing and yoga, practices that ground me and allow me to connect with my body and spirit. They remind me that I am part of something greater, and through this connection, I can facilitate healing in others.

My shaman was not only my teacher but my deepest friend. He was always amazed at my speed of learning and exploration, but he was also wise enough to remind me to rest. "Trust yourself," he would say, and those words echo in my mind whenever I feel overwhelmed. I learned to practice self-compassion and acceptance, especially during the times he wasn't available. I continued my journey, walking between worlds, embracing the light and the dark, not just as a shaman and lightworker, but as a Day Walker too.

Giving up friends and family in search of answers was a difficult choice, but I wished for nothing more than a way to find balance. My gifts never ceased, and I learned that keeping balance is what grounds me.

In a constant state of trance, I listened to nature, feeling sensitive to the energies around me. I became attuned to the weight of the soul, recognizing where people are on their journeys. My eyes, always seeking, would peek into different dimensions, revealing truths hidden from the ordinary world. Balancing two worlds is a must when being asked to embrace realities that transcend time and space; it's the only way I could get my left and right brains to work together.

The path hasn't been without its challenges. There are days when I feel overwhelmed by the energies I encounter, when the burden of others' emotions weighs heavily on my heart. But it is in those moments that I remind myself of the importance of grounding. I take time to connect with nature, allowing her to restore my balance and fortify my spirit.

I've learned to embrace the entirety of my experience, the joy and the sorrow, the light and the shadow. Each moment serves as a steppingstone toward my higher calling, a reminder that this journey is not just about me, but about the collective healing we all seek.

Explore your own journey. Embrace your calling, listen to the whispers of your heart, and trust the guidance that surrounds you. The world is waiting for your light, and every step you take brings us all closer to healing and balance.

Definition of Balance

As I reflect on my own journey, I realize that balance is like a finely tuned system. I didn't see this on my own; my deepest friend contributed. He taught me what helped him, and now it's my turn to share the wisdom that helped me. Each aspect of my being—emotional, mental, and physical—functions in harmony with the others. If one element becomes misaligned, the entire system feels the strain, and it's only a matter of time before the others start to cave under the pressure.

Through my struggles, I've learned that even when I think I don't need to focus on balance, it's crucial to perform regular maintenance. Activities like walking and engaging in creative pursuits are not just hobbies; they are essential practices that prevent the stagnation of energy within me.

When I neglect these aspects, I absorb energy that can become heavy and unyielding. This stagnation manifests as dis-ease in my body, a reminder that I must pay attention to my overall well-being. "Don't pour from an empty cup," I remind myself. I've come to understand that balance is not a destination but an ongoing journey. It requires vigilance and intention, recognizing that I must actively cultivate and nurture each aspect of my life. By doing so, I create a dynamic flow of energy that keeps me healthy, vibrant, and connected to my higher self. This understanding has transformed my relationship with balance, highlighting its significance in maintaining my overall health and harmony.

Impact on Relationships

Walking in balance has profoundly influenced my relationships, reshaping the way I connect with the people around me. I've noticed that when I am centered and grounded, my interactions are infused with a sense of peace and understanding. It's like a ripple effect; my calmness invites others to respond with openness and vulnerability.

I've experienced moments when, instead of reacting defensively in a disagreement, I could approach the situation with empathy and patience. This shift has led to deeper conversations, where we explore the roots of our feelings rather than just the surface issues.

I remember a time when a colleague and I faced a misunderstanding. In the past, my tendency would have been to escalate the tension, but because I was focusing on balance, I paused and listened intently. I could articulate my feelings without blame, and in turn, my colleague felt safe to express their own vulnerabilities. This created a space of mutual respect, where we could navigate the conflict together rather than against each other. The bonds of trust and intimacy deepened, reminding me how balance can transform relationships into sanctuaries of support and understanding.

Connection to Nature

Nature has always been my greatest teacher in finding balance. When I step outside and immerse myself in the natural world, I am reminded of the intricate dance of life. The changing seasons illustrate the beauty of cycles; winter's dormancy gives way to spring's renewal, a gentle reminder that balance is about embracing change and growth. I often find solace in watching the trees sway with the wind, their roots firmly planted yet flexible.

On walks through the woods, I feel the energy of the earth pulsating beneath my feet. It's as if the very soil invites me to reconnect, to ground myself in the present moment. Each breath I take becomes a reminder that I am part of a larger ecosystem. Observing the animals and plants thriving in their environment inspires me to align my life with nature's rhythms. I've learned that just as nature ebbs and flows, so must I. This connection not only brings me peace but also reinforces the understanding that I am never alone in my journey. The balance I seek within myself is mirrored in the world around me.

Cultural Perspectives

Exploring various cultural perspectives on balance has enriched my understanding of its significance. Each tradition offers unique insights that resonate with my personal experiences. In many Eastern philosophies, balance is often depicted through the concept of yin and yang, the idea that opposing forces are interconnected and interdependent. This duality speaks to me; it reminds me that light and darkness coexist within me, and embracing both is essential for wholeness.

I've also found wisdom in Indigenous practices that emphasize living in harmony with the earth. The teachings of reciprocity and respect for nature resonate deeply. They inspire me to cultivate a relationship with the land that acknowledges our interconnectedness. Learning about these diverse cultural perspectives broadens my understanding of balance, helping me see it not just as an individual pursuit but as a universal truth that transcends borders and beliefs. Eventually, everything connects; it's just a matter of balance.

Mindfulness Practices

In my quest for balance, I've turned to mindfulness practices that ground me in the present moment. Meditation has become a sanctuary, a time when I can observe my thoughts without judgment. Each session offers me a moment to breathe, to simply be. I've discovered that through meditation, I can cultivate a space of stillness that allows clarity and insight to emerge.

Yoga has also played a vital role in my journey. Each pose invites me to listen to my body, to honor its limitations and strengths. In those moments of stretching and flowing, I connect with my breath, anchoring myself in the here and now. I've come to realize that my body is not just a vessel but a partner in this journey toward balance. Through these practices, I'm learning to embrace the beauty of stillness, allowing it to guide me toward inner harmony.

Energy Alignment

As I delve into the energetic aspects of balance, I find myself drawn to the concept of chakras, centers of energy within the body that influence our physical, emotional, and spiritual well-being. I've learned that when these energies are aligned, I experience a profound sense of vitality and clarity. Engaging in practices like breathwork and energy healing has become essential for me, as they help me connect with my inner self and the flow of energy within. Understanding chakras has been like the adhesive that bonds all my states of being—a key component.

I've also discovered that my emotions can be powerful indicators of imbalance. When I feel stagnant or uneasy, it often signals that something within me needs attention. By tuning into these sensations, I can take proactive steps to restore harmony, whether through grounding exercises, creative expression, or simply spending time in nature. This awareness has taught me that balance is not just a state of being; it's an ongoing dialogue between my mind, body, and spirit.

Spiritual Growth

Finding balance has opened doors to my spiritual growth, allowing me to explore new dimensions of my existence. I've noticed that as I nurture equilibrium within myself, I become more attuned to my higher self, the part of me that knows my true purpose. This connection fuels my desire to delve into spiritual practices that resonate with my soul, whether through meditation, rituals, or sacred moments of reflection. In those quiet moments, I can hear my intuition guiding me, encouraging me to trust the path that unfolds before me. I've come to understand that spiritual growth is not a linear journey; it's a spiral, where each layer of understanding reveals deeper truths, which is why I say this often. Embracing balance has become a catalyst for this growth, allowing me to approach my spiritual exploration with curiosity rather than fear. The more I embrace my own light and shadow, the more I uncover the beauty of my unique journey.

Universal Principles

Through my journey, I've discovered universal principles of balance that resonate deeply with me. Concepts like yin-yang or the cycles of nature remind me that balance is a fundamental truth woven into the fabric of existence. I've started to apply these principles in my daily life, recognizing that there's beauty in embracing both light and shadow. I think of it like a battery requiring both a negative and positive charge. This understanding enriches my perspective, allowing me to approach challenges with resilience.

For instance, I often reflect on the idea that tension and

release coexist, much like the rhythm of breath. When I feel overwhelmed, I remind myself to pause, to breathe deeply, and to invite stillness into the chaos. This practice has become a lifeline, a way to reclaim my sense of balance amidst the demands of life. Recognizing these universal principles has empowered me to navigate my journey with grace and intention.

Community Impact

As I walk in balance, I've witnessed its ripple effect within my community. I've noticed how my state of being influences those around me, inspiring others to seek their own equilibrium. Each time I choose compassion over frustration or patience over haste, I contribute to a collective energy that fosters connection and understanding.

In gatherings, I see the beauty of shared experiences and the power of collective balance. When individuals come together with open hearts, the energy shifts, creating a space where healing can occur. I feel a sense of responsibility to contribute positively to this collective, knowing that my journey toward balance can inspire others to embark on their paths. Together, we can cultivate an environment where balance thrives, nurturing our community as a whole.

Global Perspective

Considering the global implications of balance, I often envision a world where individuals embrace this practice collectively. I dream of a society that prioritizes mental health, environmental sustainability, and social justice. When I think about the possibility of walking in balance on a larger scale, it feels empowering. I see myself as part of this change, encouraging others to recognize the impact their choices can have on the world.

In this vision, I imagine communities coming together to support one another, advocating for policies that promote holistic well-being. I envision educational systems that emphasize emotional intelligence and mindfulness alongside academic subjects. By embracing balance on a global scale, we can create a world where every individual feels valued, and every voice is heard.

Practical Tips

To support others in their journey toward balance, I share practical tips that have helped me along the way. Setting boundaries has been essential for me; it's a way of honoring my needs while respecting those of others. I've learned to say no when necessary, to protect my energy, and to prioritize self-care. These small acts of self-love create space for balance to flourish in our lives.

I encourage regular self-care rituals, whether it's a walk in nature, a few moments of breathwork, or simply taking time to reflect. Journaling has also become a powerful tool for me; it allows me to explore my thoughts and feelings, providing clarity and insight into my experiences. By incorporating these practices into my daily routine, I cultivate an environment where balance can thrive.

Future Vision

In my vision for the future, I see a world where individuals and communities thrive in balance. I imagine people awakening to their potential, embracing their unique gifts while working together for the greater good. I believe that by sharing our journeys and insights, we can inspire others to embark on their paths toward equilibrium. This vision motivates me to continue.

The Universal Impact of Walking in Balance

There was a time when I felt torn between light and shadow, between the fire of knowing and the quiet pull of forgetting. The world around me reflected this dissonance—chaos and stillness, destruction and creation, suffering and transcendence. I did not yet understand that all of these forces were part of a greater rhythm, a balance that stretched beyond my singular existence. But now, I see. To walk in balance is not to reject the darkness, nor to cling blindly to the light. It is to become the bridge between them, to stand at the center of the great cosmic dance and move with both. I have learned that peace is not found in avoiding the storms but in becoming the eye of them, the still point through which chaos passes without taking hold.

The impact of this choice is not mine alone to bear. I am one, but I am also many—woven into the fabric of the collective, my energy rippling outward like concentric circles on water. Every moment I choose alignment, I shift the world around me. Every breath in harmony with the greater flow sends waves of coherence into the grid. This is the path of the Day Walker: to move through the world as a tuning force, a stabilizer of frequencies, a reminder that balance is not just an idea, it is a living, breathing state of being. And as I walk, I feel the echoes of others doing the same. The pull toward unity, the subtle recalibration of energies once fractured, the unseen yet undeniable weaving of harmony into existence. The shift is not coming. The shift is here. And with each step I take, I become part of it.

How the Day Walker Contributes to Collective Awakening and Healing

There are moments when I feel the weight of the collective pressing against me, its whispers carried on unseen currents. The grief, the longing, the ache of souls who have forgotten themselves—it moves through the world like a great and ancient tide, seeking something it cannot name. But I remember. I have walked through lifetimes of forgetting, through veils so thick they felt like walls. And I have torn them down, one by one, until the truth stood before me, luminous and undeniable. I have seen the path of awakening, not as a single moment of revelation but as an unending unfolding, a spiral that deepens with every breath.

As a Day Walker, my very existence is an offering. Not a forceful demand for change, but an invitation—subtle, unwavering, undeniable. I do not wake others by shaking them from their sleep. I wake them by being awake myself. By holding a frequency so clear, so steady, that it stirs something in their souls, something ancient and familiar. Healing, too, follows this path. I do not impose it; I embody it. I let my own healing become the beacon, the resonance that calls others home to themselves.

When I choose to break my own patterns, to free myself from the chains of fear and illusion, I do not do so alone. I send ripples through the collective web, softening the bonds of those still trapped. I have come to understand that awakening is not about separation; it is about reunion. The more I rise, the more I remind others that they, too, can rise. The more I heal, the more I create space for healing to reach those who need it most. And so, I continue as a flame in the vast and growing constellation of remembrance.

Healing Through Self-Mastery

Healing is not something I do; it is something I become. It is a constant unfolding, a remembering of who I am beneath the weight of conditioning, pain, and illusion. Every step I take on this path strips away another layer, revealing the raw essence of my being. It is not easy. It is not meant to be. But I have learned that mastery is not found in avoiding the fire; it is found in walking through it, untouched by the flames.

There was a time when I thought healing meant erasing wounds, silencing the echoes of pain, becoming something other than what I was. But I know better now. Healing is not about perfection; it is about presence. It is about seeing myself fully, even in my darkest moments, and choosing to hold space for the entirety of my existence. I have faced myself in ways I never thought possible. I have stood at the edge of my own shadows and refused to turn away. I have learned when to surrender and when to rise, when to soften and when to stand firm. I have held my darkness without being consumed by it. And in doing so, I have found freedom—not from pain, but from the illusion that pain defines me.

Mastery is not a destination. It is a practice, a devotion. And as I walk this path, I know that my healing does not belong to me alone. Every lesson I integrate, every wound I alchemize, every moment of stillness I claim—it ripples outward. I become an anchor, a beacon, a reminder that peace is not found in the absence of struggle but in the mastery of my response to it. And so I walk, not above the world, but within it, carrying the light of my own becoming.

Breaking Generational Curses and Karmic Cycles

I was born into patterns that were never mine, into cycles set in motion long before I took my first breath. The weight of my ancestors' wounds, the echoes of their choices, the chains of their suffering—they were woven into me, into my very blood. For years, I carried them without question, mistaking them for my own burdens, my own fate. But I see clearly now. I am the interruption. I am the shift in the timeline. I am the soul that stands at the crossroads, staring down the ghosts of the past and declaring, *This ends with me.*

Breaking these cycles is not just about refusing to repeat them; it is about unraveling them at their core. It is about going deep into the wounds that have festered for generations and bringing light to the places no one dared to look. It is about rewriting the story, not just for myself but for those who came before me and those yet to come. I have felt the resistance, the weight of a lineage that fights to remain unchanged. The patterns run deep, the karmic threads tangled and stubborn. At times, I have felt like I am battling shadows, healing wounds I never inflicted, undoing knots that have been woven for centuries. But I persist. Because I know that every time I choose love over fear, forgiveness over resentment, freedom over the past, I alter the very fabric of my bloodline. I shift the vibration of my DNA. I set into motion a new possibility, one where pain is no longer inherited, where the cycle does not repeat, where healing is the new legacy.

This work is not just for my family; it is for the collective. Some of these cycles are not personal but karmic, woven into the fabric of existence itself. I have seen them play out again and again, across lifetimes, across realities. I have been called to end them. To break a karmic cycle is to see it for what it is—to recognize the repetition, the patterns disguised in different forms, and finally choose differently. It is rebellion, but not against the past. It is rebellion against stagnation, against the illusion that history must dictate the future. With each cycle I break, I create space for something new. A timeline unburdened. A future unwritten.

Harmonizing the Collective Grid

The universe is alive. A great, interconnected web of energy, pulsing with the thoughts, emotions, and consciousness of all beings. Whether they know it or not, every person is a note in this symphony, their vibration adding to the whole. For too long, the collective has been weighed down by dissonance—fear, division, suffering. The grid hums with their pain, their unhealed wounds rippling outward into the unseen.

But I walk differently. I do not just exist within this field. I move through it with awareness. I am not a passive note in the song; I am a tuning fork, a recalibration, a shift. My very presence alters the spaces I enter. Not because I impose my will upon them, but because I embody a frequency that reminds the grid of its own harmony. I have seen how the energy shifts when I choose love. How a room settles into stillness when I hold my center. How the wounds of the collective soften when I heal my own. My presence is a message, a ripple, an activation. I do not force others to change; I simply exist in alignment, and in doing so, I offer an invitation.

The harmonization of the collective is not a single event; it is a living process, an ongoing dance. Each awakened soul, each moment of stillness, each act of love contributes to the great balancing. As more of us rise, as more of us remember, the world begins to shift. The veil thins. The illusions fade. The song of creation hums once more in harmony. I, having played my part, continue forward, one note in the endless melody of awakening.

Answering the Call of the Higher Self

There is a voice that has always been with me, soft yet unwavering, distant yet intimately known. It speaks not in words, but in knowing, in the pull toward something greater, something vast and unnameable. For so long, I ignored it. I let the noise of the world drown it out, let doubt convince me it was nothing more than imagination. I told myself I was crazy. But the call of the Higher Self does not fade. It does not weaken. It waits, patient and eternal, for the moment I am ready to listen.

When I finally did, everything changed. Answering this call is not an easy path. It is a path of surrender and reclamation, of unlearning everything I thought I was so that I may remember what I have always been. It is a path of trust—trusting the unseen, trusting the whispers of intuition that defy logic, trusting that every challenge, every initiation, is shaping me into who I was always meant to be. I have had to let go of identities that no longer serve me. I have had to walk away from illusions that once felt safe. I have had to face the parts of myself I wished to forget. But through it all, I have discovered something far greater than comfort: I have discovered truth.

To align with the Higher Self is to step into mastery, not as something external to reach for, but as something intrinsic to embody. It is to walk with purpose, to move with intention, to recognize that every moment, every choice, is an opportunity to align with the divine flow. The deeper I go, the clearer the voice becomes. Not separate from me, but a part of me, a song I have always known, waiting to be sung.

Becoming a Beacon for Others

I do not claim to have all the answers. I am not here to dictate a path, nor to impose my truth upon another. But I know what it means to walk through the dark. I know what it means to search for something more, to feel the ache of remembering without knowing what has been lost. So, I walk not as a guide, but as a flame. A single point of light in the vast unknown.

I have seen how presence alone can shift reality, how a single act of love can ripple through time. Why stop there? I have witnessed the way one person choosing to heal, to rise, can inspire another, and another, until the whole world begins to change. I do not need to preach. I do not need to force. I only need to be, and that is enough. In being, in living my truth without apology, sovereign and in my authenticity, I become the invitation. The lighthouse in the storm. The silent reminder that awakening is possible, that healing is real, that something greater awaits beyond the veil of forgetting.

If even one soul finds their way home because they saw a reflection of themselves in my journey, then every step I have taken has been worth it. My pain and all of my challenges were not in vain. This is not just my path. It is ours.

Chapter 14 Conclusion

For as long as I can remember, people have opened up to me. They've shared their pain, their struggles, their losses. And for years, I listened, carrying their stories alongside my own. I used to compare suffering, wondering if mine was too much or if theirs was worse. But I've come to realize that pain isn't something to be measured. Whether you lose your home or your dog, whether your wounds are seen or unseen, pain is pain. And healing? Healing takes work, no matter what we are healing from.

Some days, healing feels like progress, like clarity, like air filling your lungs after being held underwater for too long. Other days, it feels like nothing at all, like you are standing in the same place, breaking in the same way, repeating the same wounds. But I promise you, even then, healing is happening. Every small act of self-kindness, every time you allow yourself to feel without judgment, every time you choose to stay instead of disappearing into the past, you are healing. Even in the moments when you don't recognize it, when it feels too slow or too small, when the weight of it all seems unbearable, you are still moving forward.

I have walked through both light and shadow, not as enemies

but as teachers. They have whispered to me in the quiet, stretched me in the darkness, and softened me in the glow. And if you've made it this far, I imagine they've done the same for you. There is no shame in our journey, no failure in our struggle. What matters is that we are here. That we keep reaching for understanding, for wholeness, for ourselves.

As we navigate this path, let us remember the power of community. We don't have to walk this journey alone. Sharing our stories, our experiences, and our vulnerabilities creates a bond that can uplift and support us. Surround yourself with those who understand your journey, who can hold space for your pain and joy alike. There is incredible strength in connection.

Let's not forget the importance of self-compassion. It's easy to be hard on ourselves during difficult times, but remember that you deserve the same kindness you would extend to a friend. Treat yourself gently, and allow yourself to rest, to feel, and to heal at your own pace.

It's essential to acknowledge that pain can lead to purpose. Our challenges often deepen our understanding of ourselves and our capacity to empathize with others. Embrace the idea that your struggles can illuminate your strengths and inspire you to help others who may be facing similar battles.

Life is a series of cycles, and both joy and pain are temporary.

On difficult days, remind yourself that it's okay to experience setbacks or to feel lost; these feelings are part of the ebb and flow of existence. Celebrate the small victories, too. Each step toward healing, no matter how minor it may seem, is a victory worth acknowledging.

So, close your eyes and take a deep breath with me. Feel the weight of all you have carried, all you have endured, all you have survived. And now, exhale. Not to release it all at once, but to make space, to allow the breath to remind us that we are still here. Still moving. Still worthy of love, of peace, of the gentleness we so freely give to others. You are not alone. You never were. The universe knows your name, and every piece of you—light and shadow—belongs. Your journey does not end here. It transforms, deepens, softens. And you, in all your vastness, will continue to unfold.

Appendix

Guides of the Soul: A Spiritual Companion

From my experience, guides often enter our lives at pivotal moments, showing us how to navigate and overcome obstacles. As they share their strengths and wisdom with us, we learn to walk in harmony, embodying their qualities and integrating them into our own lives. It's essential to remember that spirit guides come in many forms. They aren't always animals; they can be ancestors, angels, or even deities, each bringing unique insights and guidance tailored to our journeys. Embracing this diversity enriches our understanding of the support available to us from the spiritual realm.

Here is an example: Sometimes people find themselves inexplicably drawn to the majesty of wolves. Little do most people know, this attraction is often the whisper of their intuition, a connection to a wolf spirit guide revealing itself through their mind's eye. When I take a moment to explore this connection, I discover that a wolf spirit guide teaches invaluable lessons in leadership, intelligence, strategy, stamina, family bonds, protection, courage, and the importance of speaking one's truth.

Spirit guides can take various forms and serve different

purposes in spiritual beliefs. Here are some examples:

1. **Angels**: Often seen as messengers of divine guidance, angels are believed to protect and assist individuals on their spiritual journeys.

2. **Ancestors**: Many cultures honor the spirits of their ancestors, who are thought to provide wisdom, protection, and support.

3. **Animal Guides**: In shamanic practices, animals may serve as spirit guides, each representing different traits and teachings. For example, a wolf might symbolize loyalty and intuition, while an eagle could represent vision and perspective.

4. **Ascended Masters**: Spiritual figures like Buddha, Christ, or other enlightened beings are often considered ascended masters, offering guidance and wisdom from higher realms.

5. **Nature Spirits**: Elemental spirits, such as fairies or tree spirits, are believed to embody the energies of nature and can provide insight and support in connecting with the earth.

6. **Deities**: In various religious traditions, specific gods or goddesses may serve as guides, offering protection and wisdom in different aspects of life.

7. **Personal Guides**: Some individuals may connect with unique spirit guides specific to their life experiences or soul path, often appearing in dreams or meditative states.

8. **Intuitive Guides**: These can be aspects of oneself, like intuition or higher consciousness, guiding decisions and spiritual growth.

Intentional Healing: Affirmations, Chakras, Colors, and Crystals

Affirmations for the Journey

1. I am a vessel of healing and resilience, sharing my light with the world.

2. I embrace the journey of self-discovery, honoring all parts of my being.

3. I have the strength to navigate my emotions and connect deeply with others.

4. Every day, I am creating a safe space for my thoughts and feelings to flourish.

5. I am open to the wisdom of ancient traditions, integrating them into my modern life.

6. My unique voice and experiences are valuable gifts to the world.

7. I attract positive energy and nurturing connections into my life.

8. I am committed to my spiritual growth and the journey of self-love.

9. I honor my past while embracing the limitless possibilities of my future.

10. My creativity flows effortlessly, guiding me to share my story with authenticity.

11. I am worthy of love, happiness, and fulfilling connections.

12. I nurture my mind, body, and spirit with compassion and understanding.

13. I am grateful for the lessons learned and the strength gained from adversity.

14. I trust my intuition and the guidance of my higher self.

15. I am a beacon of light, inspiring others through my journey of healing.

Affirmations Specifically Focused on Chakra Healing

1. **Root Chakra (Muladhara)**: I am grounded, safe, and secure. I trust in the flow of life and feel connected to the earth beneath me.

2. **Sacral Chakra (Svadhisthana)**: I honor my emotions and embrace my creativity. I allow pleasure and joy to flow freely in my life.

3. **Solar Plexus Chakra (Manipura)**: I am confident and powerful. I trust my intuition and embrace my

personal strength.

4. **Heart Chakra (Anahata)**: I open my heart to love and compassion. I give and receive love effortlessly and unconditionally.

5. **Throat Chakra (Vishuddha)**: I express myself with clarity and confidence. My voice is strong, and I communicate my truth authentically.

6. **Third Eye Chakra (Ajna)**: I trust my intuition and inner wisdom. I see clearly and am open to new insights and perspectives.

7. **Crown Chakra (Sahasrara)**: I am connected to the divine and the universe. I embrace the flow of spiritual energy and wisdom in my life.

8. **Overall Chakra Healing**: My chakras are balanced, vibrant, and harmoniously aligned. I radiate positive energy and vitality in all aspects of my life.

9. I release any blockages that prevent me from accessing my full potential and embrace the healing energy within me.

10. With each breath, I activate my chakras, inviting healing and harmony into my being.

Remember, if our inner critic doesn't align with the

affirmations mentioned above, it's likely that a chakra is blocked. Chakra affirmations helped me recognize how I viewed myself from a trauma-based perspective rather than how my thoughts should ideally sound when in harmony. They illuminated which chakras required attention. After much practice, this perspective became ingrained in my thinking.

Colors

Colors play a significant role in chakra healing, as each chakra is associated with a specific color that corresponds to its energy and qualities. By incorporating these colors into our daily lives, we can enhance our chakra balancing and healing practices. For instance, the root chakra is linked to the color red, which signifies stability and grounding; consuming red foods like red peppers, strawberries, or beets can help energize and stabilize this chakra. The sacral chakra is associated with orange, representing creativity and pleasure; incorporating orange foods like oranges or carrots can help activate this energy. The solar plexus chakra corresponds to yellow, symbolizing personal power and confidence; foods like bananas or corn can support this chakra's energy. The heart chakra resonates with green, associated with love and compassion; consuming leafy greens or avocados can nurture this center. The throat chakra is tied to blue, which encourages communication; incorporating blueberries or blue corn can enhance this chakra's vibration. The third eye chakra is linked to indigo, representing intuition and insight; foods like blackberries or eggplant can support its energy. Lastly, the crown chakra resonates with violet, symbolizing spiritual connection; consuming foods like purple grapes or plums can help facilitate this connection. By mindfully choosing foods and surrounding ourselves with these colors, we can create an environment that fosters balance and healing within our chakras.

Chakra Corresponding Crystals

Crystals are powerful tools for chakra healing, as they resonate with the energy of each chakra, helping to balance and enhance their functions. Here's a guide to the crystals associated with each chakra:

1. **Root Chakra (Muladhara): Red Jasper**
   Properties: Red Jasper is a grounding stone that provides stability and security. It enhances vitality and promotes a sense of well-being, making it ideal for energizing the root chakra.

2. **Sacral Chakra (Svadhisthana): Carnelian**

Properties: Carnelian is a vibrant orange stone that stimulates creativity and passion. It helps to release emotional blockages and encourages a positive, joyful attitude, enhancing the energy of the sacral chakra.

3. **Solar Plexus Chakra (Manipura): Citrine**
   Properties: Citrine is a bright yellow crystal that embodies personal power and confidence. It promotes motivation, self-expression, and success, making it perfect for energizing the solar plexus chakra.

4. **Heart Chakra (Anahata): Rose Quartz**
   Properties: Rose Quartz is known as the stone of love and compassion. It opens the heart to both giving and receiving love, helping to heal emotional wounds and promote feelings of peace and harmony.

5. **Throat Chakra (Vishuddha): Lapis Lazuli**
   Properties: Lapis Lazuli is a deep blue stone that enhances communication and self-expression. It encourages clarity in thoughts and words, making it an excellent crystal for balancing the throat chakra.

6. **Third Eye Chakra (Ajna): Amethyst**
   Properties: Amethyst is a purple crystal that promotes intuition and spiritual awareness. It aids in meditation and enhances one's connection to higher

consciousness, making it ideal for the third eye chakra.

7. **Crown Chakra (Sahasrara): Clear Quartz**
   Properties: Clear Quartz is a versatile crystal that amplifies energy and intention. It enhances spiritual growth and clarity, making it an excellent stone for connecting with the divine and balancing the crown chakra.

Using Crystals for Chakra Healing

To incorporate these crystals into your chakra healing practice, you can carry them with you, meditate with them, or place them on the corresponding chakra during energy work or relaxation sessions. Setting intentions while using these crystals can enhance their effectiveness, allowing you to focus on specific areas of healing and balance in your life. By integrating these crystals into your daily routine, you can support your chakra system.

This overview provides a basic foundation for working with chakra crystals, but there is much more to explore. Each crystal has unique properties and uses that can expand your healing practice. Some crystals may be more specific in their applications, addressing particular emotional or physical issues related to each chakra. Additionally, different techniques can enhance your experience, such as crystal grids, elixirs, or incorporating sound and vibration into your practice. As you deepen your understanding of crystals and their purposes, you can discover new ways to harness their energy for more profound healing and transformation.

Identifying and Working with Triggers

Hey there, lovely readers! Let's dive into a topic that's both fascinating and a little daunting: Triggers. Now, I know what you might be thinking, "Triggers? Ugh, that sounds heavy." But fear not! We're going to explore this together with a sprinkle of lightness and a whole lot of love.

So, what exactly are triggers? In simple terms, they're like little emotional landmines, precursors. Triggers can be situations, sounds, smells, or even people that can send us spiraling into unexpected feelings. You know that feeling when a particular song comes on and suddenly, you're hit with memories of an ex? Yup, that's a trigger doing its thing!

As precursors, they're a kind of cause-and-effect relationship. If we learn all about the cause and understand how it affects us, we can begin to heal, address the cause, and turn it into transformation. This process is also a crucial part of shadow work.

Understanding triggers is super important because they can help us uncover parts of ourselves that need a little extra TLC. It is the shadow in need of light in order to harmonize. Each time we encounter a trigger, it's an invitation to get curious about what's going on inside us. It's like our own emotional GPS saying, "Hey, here's something you might want to look at!" By paying attention to our triggers, we can start to identify patterns in our emotions and reactions.

Now, here's the thing about shadow work and triggers: it's not a one-and-done deal. Expect to work through each trigger multiple times. Some answers will pop up in real time, while others might take more practice to fully understand. This often depends on the depth of the pain we endured when the trigger first occurred, as those moments can leave an imprint that we need to address later in life as we heal.

Okay, so how do we actually work with these pesky triggers? First off, I recommend keeping a little journal; this way you don't have to keep a mental list. This can be your safe space to jot down moments when you feel triggered. Ask yourself some simple questions: What happened right before I felt this way? What sensations am I noticing in my body? What thoughts are swirling in my mind? What do I need? Trust me, this can be enlightening!

When a trigger strikes, I find that mindfulness techniques work wonders. Taking a moment to breathe deeply and ground myself can really help me regain my center. During my initial shadow work, when triggered, Shai used to ask me, "Are you breathing okay right now?" This helped me understand the importance of grounding during shadow work, or in general, really. If you can, try to label your emotions as they come up. Simply saying to yourself, "I feel overwhelmed right now" can create some distance between you and that feeling.

Now, here's the fun part: reframing our triggers! Instead of viewing them as pesky roadblocks, let's see them as golden opportunities for growth. Each time you encounter a trigger, ask yourself: What can I learn from this? How can I respond differently next time? This shift in perspective can transform a challenging moment into a stepping stone on your journey.

And don't forget about your support system! Having friends, family, or a therapist to lean on can make all the difference. It's like having a trusty sidekick on your adventure—who wouldn't want that? It's okay if your support system is found in solitude; after all, like plants, growth happens in silence. Feel free to ask your spirit guides for help; believe me, they want to help us.

If needed, here's a little exercise: Create a Trigger Action Plan. This is your personal playbook for when triggers pop up. Write down your go-to steps when you feel triggered— maybe it's stepping outside for fresh air or calling a friend who always knows how to lift your spirits. Maybe it's a song that helps you lift your frequency if things get too dense. And don't forget to include self-soothing techniques, like repeating a mantra or diving into your favorite activity, a warm cup of tea, or simply, your favorite show. Remember, slow progress is always better than no progress; it truly is all about the journey.

To illustrate, let's say you're at a party, and suddenly, you feel anxious in the crowd. This might trigger memories of feeling overwhelmed in the past. Instead of letting that take over, you can remind yourself that you're in a safe space now. Maybe step outside for a breather and come back feeling refreshed.

As we explore this journey together, let's remember the importance of grounding, self-care, and self-compassion, practices I've touched on in previous chapters. These are essential tools to help us navigate triggers and foster healing. Embracing our triggers through shadow work allows us to integrate those hidden parts of ourselves and transform them into light.

In closing, remember that understanding and working through triggers is part of the beautiful journey of awakening. Embrace this process with an open heart, knowing that each trigger can lead to deeper healing and growth. So, let's dance with our triggers, learn from them, and keep moving forward together!

www.ingramcontent.com/pod-product-compliance
Lightning Source LLC
Chambersburg PA
CBHW051307120626
46547CB00015B/2128